WEB DEVELOPMENT LEVEL 1

Building Websites with HTML5 & CSS3

STEP BY STEP TRAINING

Learn by doing step by step exercises.
Includes downloadable class files that work on Mac & PC.

EDITION 2.8

Published by:

Noble Desktop LLC

594 Broadway, Suite 1202

New York, NY 10012

www.nobledesktop.com

Copyright © 2014–2017 Noble Desktop LLC

Publish Date: 10-27-2017

Table of Contents

Table of Contents

Table of Contents

Table of Contents

Table of Contents

Table of Contents

Downloading the Class Files

Thank You for Purchasing a Noble Desktop Course Workbook!

These instructions tell you how to install the class files you'll need to go through the exercises in this workbook.

Downloading & Installing Class Files

1. Navigate to the **Desktop**.

2. Create a **new folder** called **Class Files** (this is where you'll put the files after they have been downloaded).

3. Go to nobledesktop.com/download

4. Enter the code **wd-1706-19**

5. If you haven't already, click **Start Download**.

6. After the **.zip** file has finished downloading, be sure to unzip the file if it hasn't been done for you. You should end up with a **Web Dev Class** folder.

7. Drag the downloaded folder into the **Class Files** folder you just made.
   These are the files you will use while going through the workbook.

8. If you still have the downloaded .zip file, you can delete that. That's it! Enjoy.

Website Fundamentals

What Is a Website?

A website is, very simply, a collection of files in a folder. People can access the files in a website because they are hosted on a web server, accessible via the Internet or a private local area network. A website's address is known as a uniform resource locator (URL).

Webpages are delivered via Hypertext Transfer Protocol (HTTP) or HTTP Secure (HTTPS), the latter of which uses encryption and provides security for the user. The web browser renders the page content according to its HTML markup instructions.

What Is HTML?

HTML stands for **Hypertext Markup Language**. It's a standardized system for tagging content in webpages. HTML provides a way to structure text semantically into paragraphs, headings, lists, and links. It also allows images and objects like form elements to be represented on the page. Webpages link to one another with HTML markup anchors.

HTML allows computers of various platforms—Mac, Windows, etc.—to view information in essentially the same way. It helps bridge the gap between the different computer systems people use.

Even though most users will see the information as you intended, it can appear differently depending on the user's browser or operating system. For example, one person may see the text in Times, while another sees Helvetica (because they uninstalled the Times font). While the webpage may not appear exactly the same to every user, the important thing is that all users have an acceptable experience and can access the content you provide.

What Is CSS?

CSS stands for **Cascading Style Sheets**. It's a style language used to define the colors, fonts, etc. of elements in an HTML file. The main concept is that HTML files hold the content and CSS formats that content.

Because HTML and CSS are evolving languages, some users with older browsers may not be able to see effects that you include in your webpages. This is a factor to consider when designing webpages. For example, some newer CSS features may not work in a particular web browser. You have to ask yourself, can you live with the difference? If not, maybe there are only a few people using that browser so it won't be a problem. Maybe you should wait until more people use browsers that support the feature.

Website Fundamentals

The Structure of an HTML Tag

* Information in HTML documents is surrounded by tags.

* These tags are enclosed in less than (<) and greater than (>) brackets.

* If you want a heading, for example, you need to specify it as:

```
<h1>This Is My Heading</h1>
```

Note that the heading is followed by a closing tag </h1>. Most HTML tags require this ending or closing tag. If you have problems while programming HTML documents—for example, you cannot display a table correctly—it may be because you forgot to end the table with the </table> tag.

Most tags have closing tags. However, some may work even if you don't include the end tag. For example, the <p> tag, which indicates a new paragraph (and the space below it), often works without a closing </p>. Of course you should use the closing tag to ensure it works properly in all browsers. Other tags do not have closing tags at all, such as <img> (image) and
 (linebreak).

HTML tags are not case sensitive, but some things such as filenames and CSS style names are. In general, it is best practice to write all tags in lowercase.

Graphic File Formats for the Web

Graphics can be made of pixels or vectors. Pixels are square blocks that you can see if enlarged too much, whereas vectors are mathematically based perfect shapes that look great when enlarged. All the following formats are pixel-based, except for SVG.

JPEG (Joint Photographic Experts Group)

JPEG is the best format for photographic images, because it supports millions of colors and compresses color gradations without much obvious loss in quality. More compression yields a smaller file, but also creates more visible artifacts, such as loss of detail and the appearance of unsightly square blocks.

PNG (Portable Network Graphics)

PNG is the best format for pixel-based graphics with partial transparency. There are two different types of PNG:

* **PNG-24** supports millions of colors. Their pixel-perfect image quality means the file size is often large.

* **PNG-8** supports up to 256 colors, so they are typically a small file size.

GIF (Graphic Interchange Format)

GIF is the only image format that supports animation (with no coding). We rarely use GIF for static images because PNG-8 gives you the same color palette options at a file size that is 5–25% smaller.

SVG (Scalable Vector Graphics)

SVG is a vector-based format that's ideal for graphics consisting of geometric shapes, such as logos and icons. SVG scale to any size without losing clarity, so they look particularly nice on high resolution (HiDPI or Retina) displays. SVG can be used as the source (src) for an <img> tag or the SVG code can be embedded into an HTML file. SVG can be animated with JavaScript code.

Using SVG files on a website may require some configuration on the web server, which is why we won't be using them in this book. We cover SVG in our more advanced web development books.

File Naming Conventions

- When naming files, HTML documents should end with the extension **.html**

- The homepage of a website should be named **index.html**

- CSS documents should end with the extension **.css**

- File names should not use spaces or special characters. Replace spaces with hyphens.

- Use only lowercase letters when naming files (some servers are sensitive to case).

- Create a descriptive title that tells a little bit about the page content. For example: **about.html** and **contact.html** rather than **page1.html** and **page2.html**. Descriptive titles help the users understand the purpose of the page and are also good for SEO (Search Engine Optimization).

HTML vs. XHTML Syntax

HTML vs. XHTML Syntax

HTML5 is the latest HTML web standard, offering flexibility, ease-of-coding, and powerful new features. An HTML5 document can be written using HTML or XHTML syntax. There are only minor stylistic differences between the two.

We prefer HTML syntax, which is what we'll use in this training. It's even a bit less typing! If you prefer to code using XHTML syntax, refer to the list below for the few XHTML differences:

- You must specify a document type at the top of the file.

- All tags must be lowercase.

- All attributes must have quotes.

- All tags must have a close tag `<p>this is a paragraph</p>`

- If tags do not have a close tag, such as a `<br>` or `<img>` tag, they must be written as self-ending: `<br />` or `<img src="image.gif" />`

Before You Begin

Choosing a Code Editor to Work In

A nice thing about building websites is that you don't have to buy expensive software to code HTML and CSS. You can type the code into any plain text editor to get the job done. To code more quickly and efficiently, though, most web designers and developers have a code editor they prefer to use. Code editors can offer up code hints, code completion, and other handy shortcuts.

When going through this workbook you can use any code editor you prefer. Some popular choices are: Sublime Text, Atom, and Brackets. You can use whatever code editor you want, but if you don't have a preference we recommend Sublime Text. Below are instructions for getting Sublime Text, and other required software.

Downloading the Latest Browsers

All browsers handle code slightly differently, so as a web developer it's important to have all the current popular browsers installed for testing purposes.

Chrome (Mac & Windows)
* Get it free at google.com/chrome

Firefox (Mac & Windows)
* Get it free at firefox.com

Safari (Mac Only)
* To get the most recent version of Safari, you may have to update to the latest macOS.

Microsoft Edge or Internet Explorer (Windows Only)
* Update Windows to the latest version possible. You may need to upgrade to a newer version of Windows to get the most recent web browser. Microsoft Edge comes pre-installed on Windows 10 and is the latest web browser for Windows. You should at least have Internet Explorer (IE) 9.

Supported Browsers

In this workbook, we'll cover how to develop sites for modern browsers. If you discover something doesn't work in an older browser, you can often find workarounds if that browser is important to your audience.

Before You Begin

Required Software

There are many great FTP (File Transfer Protocol) clients you can use for uploading your website to a remote server, but we will use **Cyberduck** in this workbook because it is free and cross-platform.

Download and install Cyberduck from cyberduck.io (Be sure to use the download link on the left, avoiding the ad at the top.)

Recommended Software

Sublime Text is a great code editor for Mac and Windows. It has a free unlimited trial, which occasionally asks you to buy it. If you like it, you can buy it for $70.

Visit sublimetext.com and download the trial (or buy a copy) of **Sublime Text 3**.

We recommend installing some free packages (add-ons) that add great functionality. To make installing packages easier, you should first install Package Control.

Installing Package Control

1. Launch **Sublime Text**.

2. Go into the **Tools** menu and choose **Install Package Control**.

3. After a moment you should see a message telling you that Package Control was successfully installed. Click **OK**.

Installing the Emmet Package

Emmet offers shortcuts to make coding faster and easier. Here's how to install it:

1. After Package Control is installed, launch it as follows:

    • Mac: Go into the **Sublime Text** menu > **Preferences** > **Package Control**.

    • Windows: Go into the **Preferences** menu > **Package Control**.

2. Choose **Install Package**.

3. In the list that appears, start typing **emme** and **Emmet** should appear. Choose it.

4. A message will appear briefly in the bottom status bar to tell you it has been successfully installed.

Installing the SideBarEnhancements Package

The SideBarEnhancements package will allow you to hit a keystroke to quickly preview a webpage in a browser. Here's how to install it:

Before You Begin

1. Open Package Control as follows:

   - Mac: Go into the **Sublime Text** menu > **Preferences > Package Control**.

   - Windows: Go into the **Preferences** menu > **Package Control**.

2. Choose **Install Package**.

3. In the list that appears, start typing **SideBarEnhancements** and choose it when it appears.

4. A message will appear briefly in the bottom status bar to tell you it has been successfully installed.

Setting Up F12 as a Shortcut for Preview in Browser

The **SideBarEnhancements** package, in addition to other things, lets you use **F12** as a keyboard shortcut for testing a webpage in a browser. To take advantage of this, you will need to add a little code to your Sublime Text preferences.

1. Go to **nobledesktop.com/sublimetext-shortcuts**

2. Copy the following code:

```
[
    { "keys": ["f12"], "command": "side_bar_open_in_browser" , "args":{"paths":
[], "type":"testing", "browser":""}}
]
```

3. In Sublime Text, open the key binding preferences as follows:

   - Mac: Go into the **Sublime Text** menu > **Preferences > Key Bindings**.

   - Windows: Go into the **Preferences** menu > **Key Bindings**.

4. A 2-column window will open. The **Default** key bindings are on the left, and **User** (your) key bindings are on the right. In the User key bindings on the right, select and delete any code that's there.

5. In the User key bindings on the right, paste the code you just copied.

6. We recommend previewing using Chrome because we like Chrome's Developer Tools. Add the following code highlighted in bold:

```
[
    { "keys": ["f12"], "command": "side_bar_open_in_browser" , "args":{"paths":
[], "type":"testing", "browser":"Chrome"}}
]
```

7. Save and close the file.

Before You Begin

Installing the AutoFileName Package

By default Sublime Text does not suggest path and filenames. Manually typing these is tedious and it's easy to make typos. The AutoFileName package adds much needed code hints as you're typing.

1. Open Package Control as follows:

   • Mac: Go into the **Sublime Text** menu > **Preferences > Package Control**.

   • Windows: Go into the **Preferences** menu > **Package Control**.

2. Choose **Install Package**.

3. In the list that appears, start typing **AutoFileName** and choose it when it appears.

4. A message will appear briefly in the bottom status bar to tell you it has been successfully installed.

Restart Sublime Text

Some of the packages may require a restart. Quit and relaunch Sublime Text and you'll be all set!

Recommended for Mac Users

You will need to test your website to make sure that it works in Microsoft Edge and Internet Explorer (IE), because these are some of the most popular browsers. They only run on Windows, so testing can be a challenge for Mac users. Luckily, there are virtual machines that will allow you to run Windows (and, therefore, test in Edge and IE) while you're still working on your Mac.

VirtualBox is a free application that runs Windows in a virtual machine side-by-side with Mac applications. It's an ideal testing environment because you can test in all Mac and Windows browsers. Visit **virtualbox.org** to download it and learn more.

Please note that Windows is not included with VirtualBox. You will need to download your own copy of Windows. Visit **tinyurl.com/windows-vms** to download free Windows virtual machines with Edge or IE pre-installed.

Setting Up: Do This Before Other Exercises!

Creating Your Own Copy of Class Files

Throughout this workbook you will be editing class files that we have prepared for you. Instead of editing the originals, we'll have you make a copy just for yourself to edit.

1. If you have any windows open, minimize or hide them so you can see the Desktop.

2. Open the **Class Files** folder.

3. Follow the appropriate Mac or Windows instructions below:

Mac:
- Click once on the **Web Dev Class** folder to select it.

- Press **Cmd–D** to duplicate it.

- Rename the duplicate folder **yourname-Web Dev Class**.

Windows:
- Click once on the **Web Dev Class** folder to select it.

- Press **Ctrl–C** to copy it.

- Press **Ctrl–V** to paste it.

- The new copy may be at the bottom of the list of folders. Rename the folder **yourname-Web Dev Class**.

4. You now have your own set of class files to use throughout the class. Have fun!

Exercise Preview

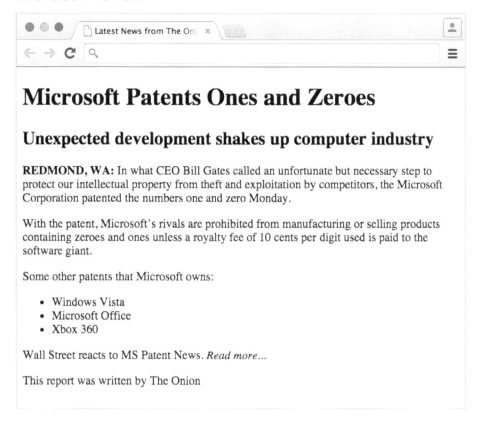

Exercise Overview

This first exercise is about as simple as it gets. You'll learn the basic syntax and the most essential HTML tags that are needed to get up and running.

Getting Started

1. Launch your code editor (**Sublime Text**, **Dreamweaver**, **Atom**, etc.). If you are in a Noble Desktop class, launch **Sublime Text**.

2. In your code editor, hit **Cmd–O** (Mac) or **Ctrl–O** (Windows) to open a file.

3. Navigate to the **Desktop** and go into the **Class Files** folder, then **yourname-Web Dev Class** folder, then **News Website**.

4. Double-click on **microsoft.html** to open it.

   NOTE: If you're using Dreamweaver, make sure you're seeing the code.

5. We've typed out some text, but it doesn't have any HTML tags yet! Add the following required tags. The code you need to type is highlighted in bold throughout the book. As you begin typing a tag, the code editor may display a list of suggested tags. For now, we recommend ignoring the code hints for opening tags.

```
<html>
<head>
    <title>Latest News from The Onion</title>
</head>
<body>
Microsoft Patents Ones and Zeroes
Unexpected development shakes up computer industry
```

6. When you type < and / most code editors will automatically type the complete closing tag for you. This is a great time-saver but you should double-check your code to make sure that your tags are closed correctly.

7. Scroll to the bottom and add the following closing tags highlighted in bold:

```
Wall Street reacts to MS Patent News. Read more...
This report was written by The Onion
</body>
</html>
```

Let's break this code down. All HTML tags sit between a less-than sign (<) and a greater-than sign (>). Most tags "wrap" around the content they describe, which means an opening/start tag and a closing/end tag must be present. The closing tag has a slash character (/) preceding the tag name.

Notice that the **<html>** tag wraps around the entire document. Inside that tag, the content is split into two sections: the **<head>** and the **<body>**. The **<head>** contains information about the document, such as its title and other data that the visitor to the site will not interact with, whereas the **<body>** contains the document's actual content that a visitor will see and interact with.

The **<title>** is meant to be an accurate and concise description of a page's content. Because it sits nested inside the **<head>** tag, it is indented. This helps to show the structure of content on the page. The **<title>** usually includes the company name and then something more specific about the document itself. Creating a concise, descriptive title is one of the most important steps of Search Engine Optimization (SEO), as the title plays a major role in most search engines' ranking scheme. Titles do not appear along with the content that shows up in the heart of the browser, at the top of the browser window in the "title bar." Titles also appear in most search engine results and in visitors' bookmarks.

8. Let's see what this page looks like in a browser. Before we preview, we need to save the file. Hit **Cmd–S** (Mac) or **Ctrl–S** (Windows).

9. Navigate to the **Desktop** and go into the **Class Files** folder, then **yourname-Web Dev Class** folder, then **News Website**.

10. **Ctrl–click** (Mac) or **Right–click** (Windows) on **microsoft.html**, go to **Open with** and select your favorite browser.

11. Take a look at the title of the document in the browser's title bar. (It may appear at either the very top of the browser or on a tab.)

12. Next, take a look at the page. The actual content of the page—which is what is wrapped inside the **<body>** tag—looks like one long paragraph of text. That's because line breaks in the code are ignored by web browsers.

    NOTE: We recommend leaving **microsoft.html** open in the browser as you work, so you can simply reload the page to see the changes as you make them in the code.

13. Return to **microsoft.html** in your code editor to continue formatting the page.

Headings

Headings help organize the content semantically so visitors can quickly skim a page. They also make your website more accessible—visually impaired visitors using a screen reader can hear the headings and jump between them in a document using a single keystroke. Headings also help search engines like Google to better understand what the page's content is about. There are six levels of headings from H1 (the most important) to H6 (the least important).

1. In your code editor, at the top of the **body** section, add the following tags highlighted in bold:

```
<body>
<h1>Microsoft Patents Ones and Zeroes</h1>
<h2>Unexpected development shakes up computer industry</h2>

REDMOND, WA: In what CEO Bill Gates called an unfortunate but necessary step
to protect our intellectual property from theft and exploitation by
competitors, the Microsoft Corporation patented the numbers one and zero
Monday.
```

2. Save the file.

3. Return to the browser and click the **Reload** button to refresh the browser window with the new code.

4. Notice that browsers render headings in bold and also render more important headings in larger fonts than less important ones. These defaults, along with the amount of spacing between the headings, can be modified using Cascading Style Sheets (CSS). For now, we are just focusing on the markup so we won't change the default look of the headings.

Coding Basics: Intro to HTML Syntax

Paragraphs

Even though there appear to be paragraphs in the provided text, the browser doesn't know where the paragraphs start and end and where to add space. We have to code that.

1. Return to **microsoft.html** in your code editor.

2. For the first paragraph, add the following opening and closing paragraph tags highlighted in bold:

```
<h1>Microsoft Patents Ones and Zeroes</h1>
<h2>Unexpected development shakes up computer industry</h2>

<p>REDMOND, WA: In what CEO Bill Gates called an unfortunate but necessary
step to protect our intellectual property from theft and exploitation by
competitors, the Microsoft Corporation patented the numbers one and zero
Monday.</p>
```

3. Wrap the remaining paragraphs, as shown below:

```
<p>With the patent, Microsoft's rivals are prohibited from manufacturing or
selling products containing zeroes and ones unless a royalty fee of 10 cents
per digit used is paid to the software giant.</p>

<p>Some other patents that Microsoft owns:</p>

    Windows Vista
    Microsoft Office
    Xbox 360

<p>Wall Street reacts to MS Patent News. Read more...</p>
<p>This report was written by The Onion</p>
```

4. Save the file.

5. Return to the browser and click the **Reload** button to refresh the browser window with the new code.

Lists

To create a bulleted list of items, you must use two tags: **<ul>** and **<li>**. The **<ul>** tag tells the browser that you want an **unordered list**, or, in other words, a bulleted list. The **<li>** tag is wrapped around the contents of each list item.

1. Return to **microsoft.html** in your code editor. Mark up a bulleted list of Microsoft's patents by adding the following code highlighted in bold (the first edit should start around line 14):

```
<p>Some other patents that Microsoft owns:</p>
<ul>
   <li>Windows Vista</li>
   <li>Microsoft Office</li>
   <li>Xbox 360</li>
</ul>

<p>Wall Street reacts to MS Patent News. Read more...</p>
```

2. Save the file.

3. Return to the browser and click the **Reload** button to refresh the browser window with the new code.

Strong & Em Formatting

The **<strong>** and **<em>** tags are semantic tags, which means they indicate that the author wishes to provide emphasis. **Strong** is rendered as bold and **em** (short for emphasis) is rendered as italic on a visual browser or in a different speaking style in a screen reader.

1. Add the following tags to mark important text (around line 9):

```
<p><strong>REDMOND, WA:</strong> In what CEO Bill Gates called an unfortunate
but necessary step to protect our intellectual property from theft and
exploitation by competitors, the Microsoft Corporation patented the numbers
one and zero Monday.</p>
```

2. Near the bottom, add the following tags to italicize the text (around line 23):

```
<p>Wall Street reacts to MS Patent News. <em>Read more...</em></p>
<p>This report was written by The Onion</p>
```

3. Save the file.

4. Return to the browser and click the **Reload** button to see the bold and italic text.

Adding the Doctype, Lang Attribute, & Meta Tags

1. Return to **microsoft.html** in your code editor.

2. Place the cursor at the very beginning of the code—directly before the html tag—and hit **Return** (Mac) or **Enter** (Windows) to get a new line on top.

3. Now add the following code highlighted in bold:

```
<!DOCTYPE html>
<html>
```

This **document type definition** (DTD) ensures that the browser renders the page in standards mode. In "standards mode" pages are rendered according to the HTML and CSS specifications, while in "quirks mode" attempts are made to emulate the behavior of older browsers.

4. Next, add the following attribute (highlighted in bold) to the html tag:

```
<!DOCTYPE html>
<html lang="en">
```

5. Briefly review the code and check for typos. Notice that **lang="en"** is written inside the html element's start tag, after the tag name but before the greater-than sign.

The **lang** attribute is used to declare the language of the page and **en** is the international standard code for English. Including this information is helpful for Search Engine Optimization (SEO) and accessibility.

> ### Attributes
>
> Many HTML tags can be enhanced with **attributes**, modifiers of HTML elements. Attributes are expressed inside the HTML element's start tag.
>
> Attributes have a name and a value. The name precedes the equal sign and the value is expressed inside double quotes.

6. Finally, add the following new line of code highlighted in bold:

```
<head>
   <meta charset="UTF-8">
   <title>Latest News from The Onion</title>
</head>
```

Meta tags can do various things, but this one says that special characters are encoded as Unicode (UTF-8). This means that special characters (like ©, ™, etc.) can be typed into the code and they'll display properly across platforms and devices.

7. Notice that, unlike most of the other tags we have used so far, both the doctype and the meta tag need not be closed. This is because these tags do not wrap around content—instead, they have a predefined behavior of their own.

8. Save the file.

9. Congratulations, you've made your first webpage! You can leave the file open so you can use it in the next exercise.

Coding Links: Absolute & Relative URLs

Exercise Preview

> **REDMOND, WA:** In what CEO Bill Gates called
> an unfortunate but necessary step to protect our
> intellectual property from theft and exploitation by
> competitors, the <u>Microsoft Corporation</u> patented the
> numbers one and zero Monday.

Exercise Overview

What would a webpage be without links? In this exercise, you'll code a few links to
learn how it's done for both external websites and other pages on your site.

1. If you completed the previous exercise, **microsoft.html** should still be open in your
   code editor, and you can skip the following sidebar. If you closed **microsoft.html**, re-
   open it now (from the **News Website** folder). We recommend you finish the
   previous exercise (1B) before starting this one. If you haven't finished it, do the
   following sidebar.

> **If You Did Not Do the Previous Exercise (1B)**
>
> 1. Close any files you may have open.
>
> 2. In your code editor, open **microsoft-ready-for-links.html** from the
>   **News Website** folder.
>
> 3. Do a **File > Save As** and save the file as **microsoft.html**, replacing the
>   older version in your folder.

The Anchor Tag & HREF Attribute

1. In the first paragraph, add the following code (highlighted in bold) around Microsoft
   Corporation. (Edits should start around line 11.)

```
<p><strong>REDMOND, WA:</strong> In what CEO Bill Gates called an unfortunate
but necessary step to protect our intellectual property from theft and
exploitation by competitors, the <a href="http://www.microsoft.com">Microsoft
Corporation</a> patented the numbers one and zero Monday.</p>
```

The markup tag for a link is the **<a>** tag, which stands for anchor. An anchor tag
doesn't do anything on its own but is quite powerful when paired with its attribute
href. Href stands for hyperlink reference. Its value is equal to the URL (uniform
resource locator) to which you'd like to link.

2. Take a moment to review the code and check for typos. Remember: attributes for an element are expressed inside the element's start tag, after the tag name but before the greater-than sign. Attributes have a name and a value. The value is expressed inside double quotes.

3. Save the file.

4. Preview **microsoft.html** in a browser.

Browser Preview Shortcuts

If you are using Sublime Text with **SideBarEnhancements** installed and have set your user key bindings in the **Before You Begin** section at the beginning of the workbook, hit **F12** (or **fn–F12** depending on your keyboard settings) to open the saved HTML document in your default browser.

This typically does not work on a Mac unless you disable/change the **Show Dashboard** shortcut in **System Preferences > Mission Control** (or **Keyboard**).

If you're using Dreamweaver, go to **File > Real-time Preview** (formerly **Preview in Browser**).

---

5. Click the link to make sure it works. Links that include the entire path (including the **http://www**) are called **absolute** links.

6. Return to **microsoft.html** in your code editor. Create another link, this time to The Onion's website (around line 23):

```
<p>Wall Street reacts to MS Patent News. <em>Read more...</em></p>
<p>This report was written by <a href="http://www.theonion.com">
The Onion</a></p>
```

7. Save the file.

8. Preview **microsoft.html** in a browser and test the new link.

   We just made two links to outside websites, but what about a link to a page in this site? We made another page (called **wall-street.html**) which is in the same folder as the page you're currently editing.

9. Return to **microsoft.html** in your code editor and right below the bulleted list, create that link by adding the code shown in bold (around line 22):

```
</ul>
<p>Wall Street reacts to MS Patent News. <a href="wall-street.html"><em>Read
more...</em></a></p>
<p>This report was written by <a href="http://
www.theonion.com">The Onion</a></p>
```

Links like this, which don't include the full path, are called **relative** links. The link is relative to the page that it is sitting in. In this case, the link will look for a page called **wall-street.html** in the same folder as our file, **microsoft.html**.

10. Save the file.

11. Preview **microsoft.html** in a browser. Take some time to test out your links.

Opening a Link in a New Browser Window/Tab

Ideally, the absolute links that go to outside webpages should open in new browser windows or tabs (depending on the user's preference). The **target** attribute allows us to tell the browser where to open the **href** (the link, or URL).

1. Return to **microsoft.html** in your code editor.

2. In the first paragraph, add the **target** attribute to the **microsoft.com** absolute link as shown below:

```
<p><strong>REDMOND, WA:</strong> In what CEO Bill Gates called an unfortunate
but necessary step to protect our intellectual property from theft and
exploitation by competitors, the <a href="http://www.microsoft.com"
target="_blank">Microsoft Corporation</a> patented the numbers one and zero
Monday.</p>
```

3. We have one more link to change. Toward the bottom add the **target** attribute to the **onion.com** link as shown below:

```
<p>This report was written by <a href="http://www.theonion.com"
target="_blank">The Onion</a></p>
```

4. Take a moment to review the code and check for typos. When an attribute is followed by another attribute, there must be a space character separating the two.

5. Save the file.

6. Preview **microsoft.html** in a browser. When you click the links, the keyword **_blank** tells the browser to open the URLs in a new browser window or tab!

7. Return to the code editor. Go ahead and close any open files. We'll be moving on to a new file next.

Adding Images

Exercise Preview

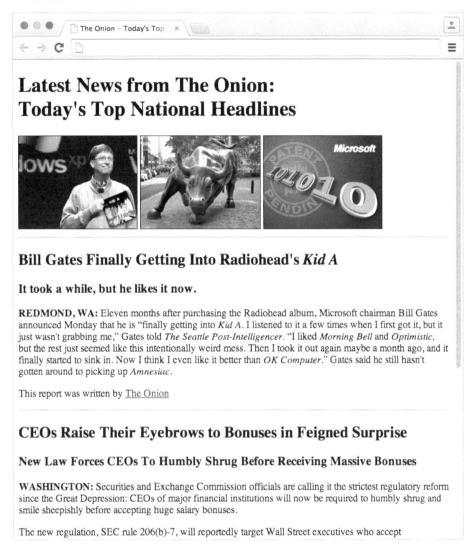

Exercise Overview

Images are another essential element of webpages. In this exercise, we'll show you how to add them to a page and include important alternative text for accessibility. You will also get to know two other tags: one for creating line breaks and another for creating the appearance of content division. What do these three tags have in common? None of them wrap around content.

1. In your code editor, hit **Cmd–O** (Mac) or **Ctrl–O** (Windows) to open a file.

2. Navigate to **Desktop > Class Files > yourname-Web Dev Class > News Website**.

1D Adding Images

3. Double–click on **index.html** to open it.

   NOTE: **index.html** is a special filename reserved for the first page (the homepage) of a website. When you go to a .com URL in a browser, the **index.html** is the first page that will be displayed.

4. Preview in a browser to get a feeling for the page. TIP: If you are using Sublime Text with **SideBarEnhancements** installed, hit **F12** (or **fn–F12**) to open your saved HTML document in your default browser. If you're using Dreamweaver, go to **File > Real-time Preview** (formerly **Preview in Browser**).

Adding a Line Break

The main heading <h1> is a bit long. A **break** tag <br> would help to make it more legible.

1. Return to **index.html** in your code editor. Add a break tag to push Today's Top National Headlines to the next line:

```
<body>
    <h1>Latest News from The Onion:<br>
    Today's Top National Headlines</h1>
```

The **
** tag, like the doctype and meta tag we added in a previous exercise, need not be closed when writing HTML-style syntax. It is a "void," or empty element in the HTML lexicon. It has no content inside of it; it simply performs its own function.

2. Save the file.

3. Return to the browser and reload the page to see the line break in the top heading.

Adding Image Files

Images are inserted into the HTML document with a single line of code. There are two main graphic file formats you will use in this class: JPEG and PNG. Please see the **Graphic File Formats** reference in the front of the workbook for more information on file formats.

1. Return to **index.html** in your code editor.

Adding Images

2. To add an image after the main heading, add the following line of code highlighted in bold (around line 10). It may not look like a single line in the book, but be sure to enter it on one line in your code.

```
<body>
    <h1>Latest News from The Onion:<br>
    Today's Top National Headlines</h1>
    <img src="images/newsthumb-bill-gates.jpg" height="145" width="190"
alt="Bill Gates, Radiohead Fan">
    <h2>Bill Gates Finally Getting Into Radiohead's
    <em>Kid A</em></h2>
    <h3>It took a while, but he likes it now.</h3>
```

3. Take a moment to review the code you just typed. The **<img>** tag requires the attribute **src** (an abbreviation of source) to call the appropriate image file. Images are typically stored in a subfolder of the website. Notice that the News Website's subfolder is named **images**, as is fairly common.

   The **alt** attribute is essential for accessibility and Search Engine Optimization (SEO). It provides "alternate" plain text content that describes the image.

   Alt Text

   The img tag's alt attribute is more commonly referred to as **alt text**. It is a brief text description of a graphic. It's used by screen readers, search engines, or is displayed if the graphic does not load.

   It is best practice to add alt text to all graphics. The only time no alt text is needed is if the graphic is purely decorative. In those rare cases, those images should be marked up so they can be ignored by assistive technology with a null alt attribute (alt="") or preferably with CSS techniques, which we'll explore later in the class.

   ---

4. Notice that the code includes a **width** and a **height** attribute. To improve the rendering speed of your webpage, it's a good practice to specify the dimensions of your image.

5. Save the file.

6. Return to the browser and reload the page to see the image.

   NOTE: Images are not actually embedded into an HTML page. The image tag is a placeholder for the linked source file and, therefore, images must be uploaded along with the HTML pages to your remote web server in order for visitors to see them.

7. Return to the code to add another image below the previous one.

1D   Adding Images

8. Type the following code highlighted in bold below (around line 11):

```
<body>
    <h1>Latest News from The Onion:<br>
    Today's Top National Headlines</h1>
    <img src="images/newsthumb-bill-gates.jpg" height="145" width="190"
alt="Bill Gates, Radiohead Fan">
    <img src="images/newsthumb-wall-street-bull.jpg" height="145" width="190"
alt="Charging Bull">
    <h2>Bill Gates Finally Getting Into Radiohead's <em>Kid A</em></h2>
```

9. Save the file.

10. Return to the browser and reload the page to see that the images sit in a line, rather than stacking on top of each other.

> **Img Is an Inline Element**
>
> Images—like text and anchor tags—are considered **inline** elements because each one goes next to the other to form a line of content. One way to stack inline elements is to place them in a container that is too narrow. Another is to change their CSS display property, which we'll explore later in the class.

11. Return to the code and add a third image below the second one you just added:

```
<img src="images/newsthumb-bill-gates.jpg" height="145" width="190" alt="Bill
Gates, Radiohead Fan">
<img src="images/newsthumb-wall-street-bull.jpg" height="145" width="190"
alt="Charging Bull">
<img src="images/newsthumb-patent.jpg" height="145" width="190" alt="Microsoft
Patent: Illustration">
<h2>Bill Gates Finally Getting Into Radiohead's <em>Kid A</em></h2>
```

12. Save the file, return to the browser, and reload the page to preview the image.

Adding Horizontal Rules

A divider line between these images and each section of content could be nice.

1. Return to the code and add the following new code—highlighted in bold—to create a horizontal rule (around line 13):

```
<img src="images/newsthumb-patent.jpg" height="145" width="190"
alt="Microsoft Patent: Illustration">
<hr size="1">
<h2>Bill Gates Finally Getting Into Radiohead's <em>Kid A</em></h2>
```

2. Save the file.

3. Return to the browser and reload the page to see the horizontal rule.

   The **<hr>** tag told the browser to draw a horizontal rule. The **size** attribute set the thickness of the rule to 1 pixel. Let's add a couple more rules for the rest of the content on this page.

4. Return to the code editor. Add another horizontal rule around line 18:

   ```
   <p>This report was written by <a href="http://www.theonion.com"
   target="_blank">The Onion</a></p>
   <hr size="1">
   <h2>CEOs Raise Their Eyebrows to Bonuses in Feigned Surprise</h2>
   ```

5. Add one final horizontal rule around line 24:

   ```
   <p>This report was written by <a href="http://www.theonion.com"
   target="_blank">The Onion</a></p>
   <hr size="1">
   <h2>Wall Street Reacts to MS Patent</h2>
   ```

6. Save the file and preview the page once more in the browser to see your final, updated content.

7. You can leave the file open in the browser and the code editor so you can use it in the next exercise.

Intro to Cascading Style Sheets (CSS)

Exercise Preview

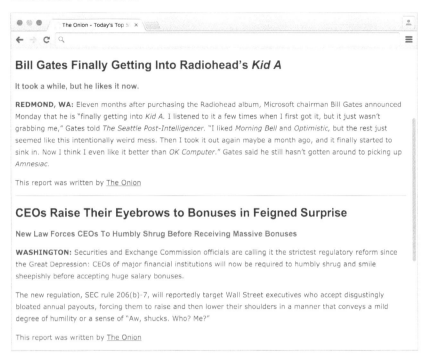

Exercise Overview

In this exercise, you'll style the page using Cascading Style Sheets (CSS). While HTML defines the type of content on the page—such as a heading, a paragraph, a list, or an image—CSS tells the browser how the content should be styled. Because CSS is not content (it just defines the style of the content) it is written in the **<head>** section rather than in the **<body>**. This is the first of many exercises on writing CSS. The focus of this exercise is on styling text (such as font, color, etc).

1. If you completed the previous exercise, **index.html** should still be open in your code editor, and you can skip the following sidebar. If you closed **index.html**, re-open it now (from the **News Website** folder). We recommend you finish the previous exercise (1D) before starting this one. If you haven't finished it, do the following sidebar.

> ### If You Did Not Do the Previous Exercise (1D)
>
> 1. Close any files you may have open.
>
> 2. In your code editor, open **index-ready-for-styles.html** from the **News Website** folder.
>
> 3. Do a **File > Save As** and save the file as **index.html**, replacing the older version in your folder.

2. Preview the file in a browser so you can see how it looks. TIP: If you are using Sublime Text with **SideBarEnhancements** installed, hit the **F12** key (or **fn–F12**) and your saved HTML document will open in your default browser. If you're using Dreamweaver, go to **File > Real-time Preview** (formerly **Preview in Browser**).

3. Notice the main heading (h1), three images, and then three "stories," each of which has a heading (h2), a subheading (h3), and some paragraphs of text.

Tag Selectors: A Good Way to Set "Default" Appearance

CSS is, in essence, a list of stylistic rules the browser must follow. Before we start writing our rules, however, we have to add an HTML tag to the page that our rules will be placed in.

1. Return to **index.html** in your code editor. Add the following bold code in the **head** section of the file, just below the **title** tag:

```
<title>The Onion - Today's Top Stories</title>
<style>

</style>
</head>
```

The **<style>** tag allows authors to embed style information in their HTML documents.

2. When applying styles, the browser first needs to know where to put them. You wouldn't hire a painter, give them some cans of paint, and have them guess where you wanted each color. In the same way you'd compile instructions for a painter (kitchen: avocado green; bedroom: soft chamois), you need to code instructions for the browser.

   The CSS selector is how the browser knows where to apply a style. The first type of CSS selector we'll learn is called a **tag selector**. Very simply, you tell the browser to find all instances of a particular HTML tag and assign a style to the element. Add the following bold **h1** tag selector inside the <style> tag:

```
<style>
   h1 {

   }
</style>
```

This rule will target all the h1's on the page.

3. Inside the h1 tag selector add the following bold code:

```
h1 {
    font-family: Arial, Helvetica, sans-serif;
    font-size: 34px;
    color: #333333;
}
```

We've added a list of styles inside the set of curly braces {} of our tag selector. These styles are called **property declarations**. You tell the browser which predefined CSS property to use (color, font-size, etc.) and set a value for the property (#333333, 34px, etc.).

A complete **rule** is officially delineated from the beginning selector (the h1 tag selector) through its closing curly brace. We have one complete rule so far. Let's see it in action.

NOTE: We recommend formatting your CSS so that each **property declaration** is indented and on its own line. Your code editor may do this for you as you type. If your code editor doesn't do this, you can manually tab in each property declaration, though this is done purely for legibility reasons. The browser does not need this formatting in order to understand the code and apply the styles—it's just much easier to read, particularly when you're first learning CSS.

4. Save the file.

5. Return to the browser and reload the page to see that the heading at the top has changed. Awesome!

6. Return to **index.html** in your code editor.

1E

Intro to Cascading Style Sheets (CSS)

7. Inside the `<style>` tags, below the **h1** style, add styles for the heading 2 and heading 3 tags (type only the new code that is highlighted in bold):

```
h1 {
    font-family: Arial, Helvetica, sans-serif;
    font-size: 34px;
    color: #333333;
}
h2 {
    font-family: Arial, Helvetica, sans-serif;
    font-size: 24px;
    color: #423000;
}
h3 {
    font-family: Arial, Helvetica, sans-serif;
    font-size: 16px;
    color: #556d7d;
}
</style>
```

The Font-Family Property

You most likely noticed that the value you wrote for the **font-family** properties is actually a list of fonts—a "wish list" of sorts. The first font will be applied if it's available on the user's computer. The second, third, or any following fonts will only be used if the preceding font is not available.

Units of Measure for Type in CSS

Even though it's possible to choose **points** for font size, it is better to use **pixels** to make sure fonts will display the same size across browsers and platforms (Mac, Windows, iOS, Android, etc.).

Pixels are a proper form of measurement for our current media (the screen), while **points** are a print measurement. Some web developers like to use **ems**. They are a proportional measurement and can involve some math to figure out your type sizes. To get started, we'll use pixels because they are easier.

8. Save the file.

9. Return to the browser and reload the page again to see your new heading styles. You have effectively coded styles that redefine the look of all elements in the page that have been tagged as h1, h2, or h3.

10. Let's add another rule. Return to your code editor.

42   WEB DEVELOPMENT LEVEL 1 • COPYRIGHT NOBLE DESKTOP

Intro to Cascading Style Sheets (CSS)

11. Below the **h3** rule, add a rule for all paragraphs (type only the new rule that is highlighted in bold):

```
h3 {
    font-family: Arial, Helvetica, sans-serif;
    font-size: 16px;
    color: #556d7d;
}
p {
    font-family: Verdana, sans-serif;
    font-size: 14px;
    line-height: 24px;
    color: #4a4c4d;
}
</style>
```

NOTE: The line-height property defines the amount of space above and below inline elements. This property is most often used to set the leading—or distance—between lines of text. Readability can be dramatically improved by increasing line-height, particularly if the lines of text are long.

12. Save the file.

13. Return to the browser and reload the page. What a difference!

> ## Hexadecimal Color Codes
>
> Color for the web can be expressed as a 6-digit hexadecimal value that represents RGB color values: the first 2 digits are red, the next 2 green, and the last 2 are blue. Hexadecimal code must be preceded by a # sign: **#00ff33**
>
> The letters in hex values are not case sensitive—they can be written in either upper or lowercase.

CSS Class Selectors

Exercise Preview

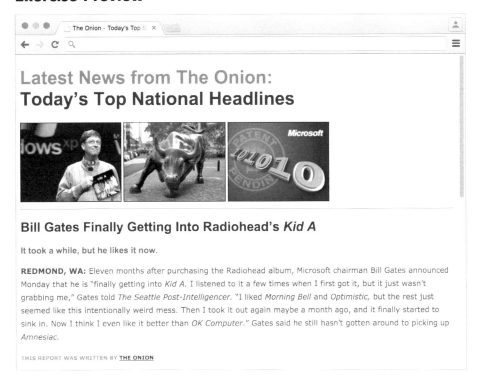

Exercise Overview

In the previous exercise you learned that CSS tag selectors are quick, easy, and efficient but they target all instances of a tag. What if you want a certain paragraph to look different, for instance? In this exercise you'll learn how to use the **class selector** to override a tag selector anywhere you like.

1. If you completed the previous exercise, **index.html** should still be open in your code editor, and you can skip the following sidebar. If you closed **index.html**, re-open it now (from the **News Website** folder). We recommend you finish the previous exercise (1E) before starting this one. If you haven't finished it, do the following sidebar.

> ### If You Did Not Do the Previous Exercise (1E)
>
> 1. Close any files you may have open.
>
> 2. In your code editor, open **index-ready-for-classes.html** from the **News Website** folder.
>
> 3. Do a **File > Save As** and save the file as **index.html**, replacing the older version in your folder.

2. Preview the file in a browser so you can see how it looks.

   TIP: If you're using Sublime Text with **SideBarEnhancements** installed, hit the **F12** key (or **fn–F12**) to open your HTML file in the default browser. If you're using Dreamweaver, go to **File > Real-time Preview** (formerly **Preview in Browser**).

Class Selectors: Making Exceptions to the Defaults

Class selectors can be assigned to any tag and used as few or as many times as you wish. There are no predefined names for class selectors. You come up with a custom name for them according to their functionality.

When writing a class selector, you use the period, or **dot** (.) notation prior to the name of the selector to alert the browser to the fact that this is not a predefined tag selector.

1. Back in the code editor, under the **p** style, add the following bold code. (Remember: the dot before **author** is there on purpose—that's what makes it a **class** selector!)

```
p {
    font-family: Verdana, sans-serif;
    font-size: 12px;
    line-height: 20px;
    color: #4a4c4d;
}
.author {
    font-size: 10px;
    text-transform: uppercase;
    font-weight: bold;
    color: #a18f81;
}
</style>
```

2. Now that the rule is created, you must tell the browser where to apply it. You can add the **class attribute** to any HTML tag to assign a style to the content associated with that specific tag. To assign the rule, find the following code (should be in line 46) and add the class attribute and value shown in bold here:

```
<p class="author">This report was written by <a href="http://www.theonion.com" target="_blank">The Onion</a></p>
```

3. Take a moment to check the code for typos. Note that the value of **class** is simply **author**. You do not type the dot preceding a class name when you assign its value in the HTML.

   Now that you have assigned the rule, the idea of a class selector might make a bit more sense: you are essentially telling the browser that this paragraph isn't just any old ordinary paragraph but a special "class" of paragraph.

4. Save the file.

5. Return to the browser and reload the page. Look for the sand brown, uppercase text: **THIS REPORT WAS WRITTEN BY THE ONION**. How classy!

6. Return to **index.html** in your code editor.

7. Classes can be reused as many times as needed. The second story has a paragraph that could also use the **author** class. Around line 52, find the paragraph that begins, **This report was written**… and add the following code shown in bold:

```
<p>The new regulation, SEC rule 206(b)-7, will reportedly target Wall Street
executives who accept disgustingly bloated annual payouts, forcing them to
raise and then lower their shoulders in a manner that conveys a mild degree of
humility or a sense of "Aw, shucks. Who? Me?"</p>
<p class="author">This report was written by <a href="http://www.theonion.com"
target="_blank">The Onion</a></p>
<hr size="1">
```

8. Down a bit further in the code—around line 58— there's one more story that could use an **author** paragraph. Add the following code shown in bold:

```
    <p class="author">This report was inspired by, but not written by <a
href="http://www.theonion.com" target="_blank">The Onion</a></p>
</body>
</html>
```

9. Save the file.

10. Return to the browser and reload the page to see that the author style applies to multiple paragraphs on the page.

The Span Tag

Let's style the first part of the main heading—Latest News from the Onion—so its color is "muted" a bit. We can make it a slightly lighter gray than the rest of the heading. Let's create a class selector for this purpose.

1. Return to **index.html** in your code editor.

2. Under the **.author** style, add the following bold code:

```
.author {
   font-size: 10px;
   text-transform: uppercase;
   font-weight: bold;
   color:#a18f81;
}
.heading-muted {
   color: #888888;
}
</style>
```

NOTE: Class names are case sensitive and cannot contain spaces or special characters aside from hyphens or underscores to separate a multi-name class. We are using a hyphen here, as it has become an industry standard.

3. Now we need to assign this class to the first part of the h1 tag. The one catch is that classes are assigned to entire HTML tags, but we'd like to target just a portion of the content inside the tag. Luckily, there is a special tag in HTML that is used for the specific purpose of assigning styles to small areas of content: **<span>**.

Find the h1 tag around line 40 and add the following bold code:

```
<h1><span class="heading-muted">Latest News from The Onion:</span><br>
   Today's Top National Headlines</h1>
```

4. Save the file.

5. Return to the browser and reload the page to see your span tag and class selector in action. Sweet!

6. Feel free to keep index.html open in the browser. You'll continue with this file in the next exercise.

_____

Exercise Preview

Exercise Overview

You have already seen that CSS, when combined with the HTML tags that have been covered so far in this workbook, can style a page so that the type is a bit more elegant. However, in order to have full control over real page layout, another HTML element can come in quite handy: the **div**.

Div is short for "division". Wrapping content in div tags allows authors to create sections of content that are grouped together and styled via CSS rules.

2B The Div Tag & Basic Page Formatting

1. If you completed the previous exercise, **index.html** should still be open in your code editor, and you can skip the following sidebar. If you closed **index.html**, re-open it now (from the **News Website** folder). We recommend you finish the previous exercises (1D–2A) before starting this one. If you haven't finished them, do the following sidebar.

If You Did Not Do the Previous Exercises (1D–2A)

1. Close any files you may have open.

2. In your code editor, open **index-ready-for-divs.html** from the **News Website** folder.

3. Do a **File > Save As** and save the file as **index.html**, replacing the older version in your folder.

Wrapping Content in a Div

1. Preview the file in a browser so you can see how it looks. Take a moment to click and drag the edge of the browser window in and out to resize the window. Notice how all the content, including the images, simply wrap to the edge of the browser window. This isn't all that problematic for the more narrow window size, but if you make the window rather wide, the content stretches out to a point where it is incredibly hard to read.

   The **<div>** tag will allow us to gain more control over the layout.

2. Return to **index.html** in your code editor.

3. To wrap a div tag around all the content of the document, type the following opening tag (highlighted in bold) just below the opening body tag in your file. It should be somewhere around line 40:

   ```
       </style>
   </head>
   <body>
       <div>
           <h1><span class="heading-muted">Latest News from The Onion:</span><br>
               Today's Top National Headlines</h1>
   ```

4. Close the tag just above the closing body tag (around line 63), as shown:

   ```
           <p class="author">This report was inspired by, but not written by <a
   href="http://www.theonion.com" target="_blank">The Onion</a></p>
       </div>
   </body>
   </html>
   ```

5. If you haven't indented the lines in between the opening and closing **div** tags, do so now. This will make your code vastly more legible. Most code editors have keystrokes for indenting lines of code so you can do this quickly.

Code Indentation Shortcuts

Highlight the line(s) of code and try one of these keystrokes:

- **Tab** to indent. **Shift–Tab** to unindent.

- **Cmd–]** (Mac) or **Ctrl–]** (Windows) to indent.
  Cmd–[(Mac) or **Ctrl–[** (Windows) to unindent.

- Dreamweaver: **Cmd–Shift–>** (Mac) or **Ctrl–Shift–>** (Windows) to indent.
  Cmd–Shift–< (Mac) or **Ctrl–Shift–<** (Windows) to unindent.

---

6. Save the file and preview it in a browser. There should be no discernible change as of yet. We need to use CSS to tell the browser how to style the div.

Creating a Fixed Width Layout

1. Return to **index.html** in your code editor.

2. In the **style** tag, add the following new rule (highlighted in bold) to the code. Place it between the paragraph and **.author** rule (around line 28), like so:

```
p {
    font-family: Verdana, sans-serif;
    font-size: 12px;
    line-height: 20px;
    color: #4a4c4d;
}
div {
    width: 580px;
}
.author {
    font-size: 10px;
    text-transform: uppercase;
    font-weight: bold;
    color: #a18f81;
}
```

NOTE: As a best practice, coders typically organize their CSS so that all their tag selectors are together at the top. Remember that tag selectors define the way these elements should look in general. Class selectors can then be used to target the elements more specifically if the general rules need to be overridden.

3. Save the file.

4. Return to the browser and reload the page to see your newly formatted content. Make sure to resize the browser to see how the content is now fixed within a 580 pixel-wide container.

Creating Contrast with Background-Color

1. Return to **index.html** in your code editor.

2. In the **style** tag, add the following new rule (highlighted in bold) to the code. Place above all the other rules (around line 7), like so:

```
<style>
   body {
      background-color: #bdb8ad;
   }
   h1 {
      font-family: Arial, Helvetica, sans-serif;
      font-size: 32px;
      color: #333333;
   }
```

3. Save the file.

4. Return to the browser and reload the page to see that the color affects the entire page background—it sits behind all the content.

   The body element is, in some ways, like the canvas or artboard of your document. Styles that you declare inside a rule for the body tag will allow you to shape the color of the page and how much space (margin) the browser will place between the content and the edge of the browser window, for instance.

5. Return to **index.html** in your code editor.

6. We can add more contrast to the content to really make it pop. In the **style** tag, find the rule for **div** and add the following property declaration (in bold):

```
div {
   width: 580px;
   background-color: #ffffff;
}
```

7. Save the file.

8. Return to the browser and reload the page to see that the color affects only the content inside the div tags. The body of the document has a different color that sits neatly behind the div.

Adding Padding Inside the Div

1. The content is very close to the edges of the browser and could use some **padding** (space between an HTML element's content and its edge) to make it more legible. Return to **index.html** in your code editor and add the following property declaration (in bold) to your rule for **div**:

```
div {
    width: 580px;
    background-color: #ffffff;
    padding: 20px;
}
```

   This property declaration sets 20 pixels of padding on all four sides of the element—top, right, bottom, and left—equally.

2. Save the file.

3. Return to the browser and reload the page to see the improved formatting.

Centering Content

1. Return to **index.html** in your code editor and add the following two new property declarations (in bold) to your rule for **div**:

```
div {
    width: 580px;
    background-color: #ffffff;
    padding: 20px;
    margin-left: auto;
    margin-right: auto;
}
```

2. Save the file.

3. Return to the browser and reload the page to see how the browser magically centers your div in the browser window.

   How does it work? Well, it's not magic, it's math! You set a width for the div element and then specified that you wanted the margins on the left and the right to be "automatic," so the browser makes them equal to one another. The effect horizontally centers the div with respect to the edges of the body of the document.

4. Take a moment to make the browser window more narrow. Notice that, at a smaller width, you have to horizontally scroll to see all the content on the page. This is not ideal but, going forward, we will address creating more flexible, fluid layouts that work a bit better in both large and small windows.

Adding a Border

1. Return to **index.html** in your code editor and add the following three new property declarations (in bold) to your rule for **div**:

```
div {
    width: 580px;
    background-color: #ffffff;
    padding: 20px;
    margin-left: auto;
    margin-right: auto;
    border-width: 1px;
    border-style: solid;
    border-color: #959485;
}
```

NOTE: Our **border-style** property tells the browser to render all sides of the border as a solid line. Other possible values include dashed and dotted.

2. Save the file.

3. Return to the browser and reload the page to see that your 1-pixel-wide, solid, caramel brown border nicely offsets the div and its content from the page background, creating a more organized look for the page.

CSS Clean-up: Shorthand & "DRY"

Instead of specifying the width, style, and color for the border as three separate property declarations, CSS has a method of "shorthand" we can use to write a border style more elegantly.

1. Return to **index.html** in your code editor.

2. Edit your rule for **div** as shown below. Note that, instead of three lines of code to describe the border properties, one **border** declaration can be written like so:

```
div {
    width: 580px;
    background-color: #ffffff;
    padding: 20px;
    margin-left: auto;
    margin-right: auto;
    border: 1px solid #959485;
}
```

3. While we're cleaning up our CSS, take note of how often we declare **font-family: Arial, Helvetica, sans-serif;**

   A core principle of coding and software development is **DRY**, which stands for "don't repeat yourself." It is essential to try to avoid redundancies and write the most elegant code possible.

   It's possible to declare our default font-family just once—in the body rule—and have all elements, because they sit inside the body tag, inherit this property.

4. Edit your CSS rules as shown below. You can delete the **font-family** declaration from **h1**, **h2**, and **h3** and, instead, place it inside the **body** rule:

```
body {
    font-family: Arial, Helvetica, sans-serif;
    background-color: #bdb8ad;
}
h1 {
    font-size: 32px;
    color: #333333;
}
h2 {
    font-size: 20px;
    color: #423000;
}
h3 {
    font-size: 16px;
    color: #556d7d;
}
```

5. Save the file.

6. Return to the browser and reload the page. The code is leaner and more elegant, but your changes did not alter the final style of the elements on the page. Success!

Using Browser Developer Tools

Exercise Preview

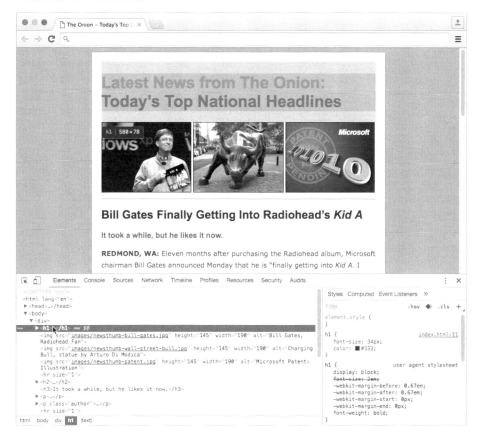

Exercise Overview

In this exercise, we'll introduce you to browser developer tools. All major browsers have built-in tools that allow you to access the code with precision. These tools allow you to review and edit the HTML and CSS on-the-fly to update your design and fine-tune your styles with greater ease.

The steps in this workbook are written for Chrome's DevTools, but the tools found in other browsers often work similarly.

2C

Using Browser Developer Tools

1. If you completed the previous exercise, **index.html** should still be open, and you can skip the following sidebar. If you closed **index.html**, re-open it now. We recommend you finish the previous exercises (1D–2B) before starting this one. If you haven't finished them, do the following sidebar.

> **If You Did Not Do the Previous Exercises (1D–2B)**
>
> 1. Close any files you may have open.
>
> 2. In your code editor, open **index-ready-for-dev-tools.html** from the **News Website** folder.
>
> 3. Do a **File > Save As** and save the file as **index.html**, replacing the older version in your folder.

Using Chrome's DevTools

1. Preview index.html in **Chrome**.

2. To open the DevTools, **Ctrl–click** (Mac) or **Right–click** (Windows) on the page and choose **Inspect**.

   The DevTools window has several groups of tools organized into tabbed panels. By default, you should see that the **Elements** panel is open. This is the perfect place to be. In this section of the panel, you can inspect an HTML element and see its precise markup. Another section of the panel will show the corresponding CSS for the element you have selected.

3. We want the DevTools docked to the bottom. If the DevTools are docked to the right side of the browser window, at the top right of the DevTools panel click the ⋮ button and then choose **Dock to bottom** as shown below:

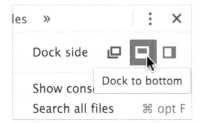

4. Start by investigating the left side of the panel to see the HTML markup. Here, you can view, access, and edit all elements in the **DOM tree**, which is a fancy way of saying you can see the structure of your document and the way each HTML element is nested inside another. (DOM is short for Document Object Model.)

5. Take the time to mouse over the tags. As you do so, you should see the element highlighted in the browser window on top, along with a tooltip that shows the HTML element's width and height.

6. While you're here, also take note of the little arrows that can be opened and closed to show the contents of the HTML elements. Experiment a little by opening up the **<h1>** tag to see the content. Notice the nested **<span>** and **
** tags. It is helpful to know that the <h1> is considered the parent element and the <span> and <br> are, by that token, child elements within the <h1>. Following this logic, the <span> and <br> elements are siblings according to the structure of the DOM tree.

7. Double–click on the text inside the **\<h1\>** element and feel free to type out some new text, as shown below:

8. Hit **Return** (Mac) or **Enter** (Windows) to see the change in the browser above the DevTools. Wow! Easy.

   Play around for a bit and have fun. Don't worry: the changes you make to your content in the DevTools are temporary. You need to modify the content in your actual HTML file to save the changes.

9. Reload the browser to see the original content once more.

10. Click on the **\<div\>** tag in the DevTools window and take a glance over to the right side to see the **Styles** associated with this element.

11. Take a moment to mouse over the properties for the **div** rule. You should see **checkboxes** appear next to each property declaration. Try checking and unchecking the properties to see how you can temporarily disable and re-enable the property in the browser. When a property is disabled, it will appear with a strike-through:

```
div {
    ☑ width: 580px;
    ☐ background-color: ☐#fff;
    ☑ padding: ▶20px;
    ☑ margin-left: auto;
    ☑ margin-right: auto;
    ☑ border: ▶1px solid ▉#959485;
}
```

12. Find the **border** property. Click on the value that's there (1px solid #959485) and notice that you can edit this value. Type in **2px dashed #f00** or any other width, style, or color to see how the browser previews this change:

```
div {
    width: 580px;
    background-color: □#fff;
    padding: ▶20px;
    margin-left: auto;
    margin-right: auto;
    border: 2px dashed #f00;
}
```

NOTE: Other possible values for border styles are: **dotted, double, groove, ridge, inset and outset**. You can also override a border style by setting the value to **none** or **hidden**.

13. Play around for a bit and have fun. Remember: the changes you make to the code in the DevTools are temporary. You need to note the new values and then code them into your actual CSS file to save the changes.

14. Find the **width** property and click on the value to highlight it. Use the **Up Arrow** on your keyboard to increase the value **1** pixel at a time. If you add the **Shift** key, you can modify the value **10** pixels at a time. Use the **Down Arrow** to decrease the value.

```
div {
    width: 618px;
    ☑ background-color: □#fff;
    ☑ padding: ▶20px;
    ☑ margin-left: auto;
    ☑ margin-right: auto;
    ☑ border: ▶1px solid ■#959485;
}
```

15. Watch how the width is updated live in the browser window. Reload the browser to return to the originally assigned values.

We don't want to actually modify this element's width or border, but this gives you a sense of how the DevTools (or an inspector in another browser) can help you refine the values of your CSS and get immediate visual feedback on your changes.

Let's put what we've learned to some use in fine-tuning this particular page.

Fine-Tuning Margins in the Main Heading

1. Take a look at the main heading of the page (Latest News from the Onion: Today's Top National Headlines) and notice that the space around the heading is uneven. There's way more space above the heading than on the left. This space could be balanced a bit better.

2. Look down to the DevTools window. On the left side, find the **<h1>** tag.

3. Mouse over the **<h1>** tag and, as you do so, take a look at the way it is highlighted in the browser window above. You should see an orange-colored highlight above and below the header. The orange color indicates that there is a margin present:

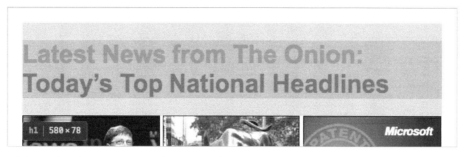

4. Click on the the **<h1>** tag in the DevTools window to select it. You will now see the **Styles** associated with the **h1** on the right side of the DevTools window:

5. You'll notice that we did not add any margin to h1 in our style sheet in index.html but, just below those rules, you'll see rules added by a **user agent stylesheet**. This indicates styling the browser does by default. All browsers add margin to the top and bottom of paragraphs, headings, and lists. Let's override this.

6. In the **Styles** section of DevTools, to edit our rule for **h1**, click once inside the opening curly brace:

```
h1 {
    | ;
    ☑ font-size: 34px;
    ☑ color: ■#333;
}
```

7. Type **margin-top** and hit **Tab**. Then type **5px**.

```
h1 {
    margin-top: 5px;
    ☑ font-size: 34px;
    ☑ color: ■#333;
}
```

8. Feel free to use the **Up Arrow** and **Down Arrow** on your keyboard to modify the margin height. You'll notice that the heading looks best when **margin-top** is set to **0px**. Let's add this property declaration to our code to lock it in.

9. You should still have **index.html** open in your code editor. If not, open it now.

10. Find your **h1** rule (around line 11) and add the following new property declaration, as shown below in bold:

```
h1 {
    margin-top: 0;
    font-size: 34px;
    color: #333333;
}
```

NOTE: In CSS, you must always specify a unit of measurement when coding a numeric value. This is why we typically have px clearly stated after the numeric value we coded. On the other hand, if the value you wish to code is 0 (zero), you need not specify px or otherwise. Zero is zero, regardless of the unit of measurement.

11. Save the file.

12. Return to the browser and reload **index.html** to see your final change to the code.

Exercise Preview

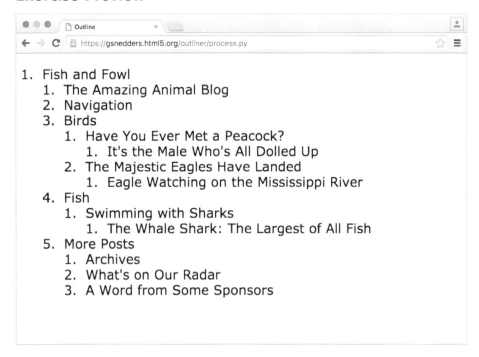

Exercise Overview

The World Wide Web Consortium (W3C) is an international community where Member organizations, a full-time staff, and the public work together to develop Web standards. Among other tasks, the W3C works hard to standardize and improve languages like HTML and CSS.

In a prior exercise, we used the div tag to group together the content so we could have more control over how to style it. In an earlier version of HTML, this was the only tag we had at our disposal for creating sections of content in the page. In the latest W3C specification of HTML—HTML5—we can make use of semantic tags to natively describe the contextual function of the element. This is beneficial not just to designers and developers but for screen readers and search engines. Good for humans and good for robots!

Getting Started

1. In your code editor, hit **Cmd–O** (Mac) or **Ctrl–O** (Windows) to open a file.

2. Navigate to **Desktop > Class Files > yourname-Web Dev Class > Structural Semantics**.

3. Double–click on **semantic-elements.html** to open it.

4. Before we start tagging the content, let's get acquainted with it. Preview **semantic-elements.html** in a web browser.

5. Scroll down the page and scan the content. In particular, note the three headings in the middle of the page. There are two that introduce articles about birds (Peacocks and Eagles) and one about fish (Sharks). This is the primary content for the page.

6. Switch back to **semantic-elements.html** in your code editor.

The Outline Algorithm

Every webpage has an outline. It's similar to a table of contents. In the provided webpage, we've marked up some text and tagged the basic content, but, aside from the heading levels (h1 through h6) the page does not have as much semantic structure as it could. Let's take a look at the document outline and see how it can be improved.

There are many online tools and browser extensions that make use of the document outline algorithm to help you visualize and improve a document's outline. We'll use one created by developer Geoffrey Sneddon.

1. Open a web browser and go to: gsnedders.html5.org/outliner

2. Under **Input HTML**, click the **Browse** or **Choose File** button (the button name differs between browsers).

3. Navigate to **Class Files > yourname-Web Dev Class > Structural Semantics**.

4. Double–click **semantic-elements.html** to choose it.

5. Click the **Outline this!** button just below the file.

The outline you see currently reflects only the basic heading tags (h1 through h6) for page structure. In HTML 4, this was the only way to outline a document. HTML5 semantic elements (tags) allow us to more finely tune the outline and create a semantic structure that is more friendly for both developers and machines to read. Let's investigate!

The Header

1. Let's begin with the **header** element. Switch back to your code editor.

2. Find these two lines of code (starting around line 8):

```
<h1>Fish and Fowl</h1>
<h2>The Amazing Animal Blog</h2>
```

3. As shown below, wrap these two lines of code in a **header** tag.

   TIP: If Emmet is installed in your code editor, you can quickly wrap a tag around a selection using a keystroke. Select the code you want to wrap and hit **Ctrl–W** (Mac) or **Ctrl–Shift–G** (Windows). Then type in the name of the wrapper (which in this case is **header**) and hit **Return** (Mac) or **Enter** (Windows).

```
<header>
    <h1>Fish and Fowl</h1>
    <h2>The Amazing Animal Blog</h2>
</header>
```

   As you may have guessed, this tag defines the main headings of a page or section. It can also contain a logo and/or a navigational table of contents.

   NOTE: Because semantic tags allow us to partition our content logically, each discrete section can have its own h1, according to the W3C specification for HTML5. For accessibility purposes, however, it is a best practice to only have one h1 per page until screen reader technology supports multiple h1 tags.

Proper Semantics for Nav Elements

1. Next up is the navigation content. Find the following code around line 13:

```
<h2>Navigation</h2>
    <a href="#">About Us</a>
    <a href="#">Our Mission</a>
    <a href="#">Contact Us</a>
```

2. These are links to navigate the site, so let's wrap a **nav** tag around this content, as shown below:

```
<nav>
  <h2>Navigation</h2>
    <a href="#">About Us</a>
    <a href="#">Our Mission</a>
    <a href="#">Contact Us</a>
</nav>
```

   NOTE: The links here are purely for demonstration purposes; we don't really have actual pages to link to as yet. Setting the value of the **href** to **#** is a standard way to create a placeholder link. It comes in handy as a way to style your links before you have the rest of the site created.

3. While we're here, let's mark up the nav element with some additional semantic value. Traditionally, web developers present navigation links as list items inside an unordered list. This makes good sense. After all, you're essentially presenting a list of links to your visitor. Let's mark this up accordingly.

4. Edit the nav contents to wrap an unordered list around the links:

```
<nav>
    <h2>Navigation</h2>
    <ul>
        <a href="#">About Us</a>
        <a href="#">Our Mission</a>
        <a href="#">Contact Us</a>
    </ul>
</nav>
```

5. Now wrap each link in a list item, as follows:

```
<nav>
    <h2>Navigation</h2>
    <ul>
        <li><a href="#">About Us</a></li>
        <li><a href="#">Our Mission</a></li>
        <li><a href="#">Contact Us</a></li>
    </ul>
</nav>
```

6. Save the file.

The Article, Aside, & Footer Elements

1. Below the nav, find the first blog post. The **article** element is ideal for this type of content.

   According to the W3C HTML5 spec, "The article element represents a self-contained composition in a document, page, application, or site and that is, in principle, independently distributable or reusable, e.g. in syndication. This could be a forum post, a magazine or newspaper article, a blog entry, a user-submitted comment, an interactive widget or gadget, or any other independent item of content."

2. As shown below, wrap the following lines of code in an **article** tag:

```
<article>
    <h2>Have You Ever Met a Peacock?</h2>
    <h3>It's the Male Who's All Dolled Up</h3>

    ( CODE OMITTED TO SAVE SPACE )

    <p>Source: <a href="http://en.wikipedia.org/wiki/Peafowl">Wikipedia</a></p>
</article>
```

3. Wrap the **article** tag around the **two** remaining articles. The code should look like this when you are finished:

```
<article>
    <h2>The Majestic Eagles Have Landed</h2>
    <h3>Eagle Watching on the Mississippi River</h3>

    ( CODE OMITTED TO SAVE SPACE )

    <p>Source: <a href="http://en.wikipedia.org/wiki/Eagle">Wikipedia</a></p>
</article>

<article>
    <h2>Swimming with Sharks</h2>
    <h3>The Whale Shark: The Largest of All Fish</h3>

    ( CODE OMITTED TO SAVE SPACE )

    <p>Source: <a href="http://en.wikipedia.org/wiki/
Whale_shark">Wikipedia</a></p>
</article>
```

Let's next mark up the sidebar of additional posts and links. The **aside** element is used to indicate tangential, additional content. The W3C chose "aside" over "sidebar" not to be fancy and Shakespearean, but because it more accurately describes the semantic value of the content rather than the content's position on the page. Sidebars are often placed off to the left or the right but then they are moved to the bottom of the main content for a mobile layout. Aside is a more flexible term.

4. As shown below, wrap the following content in an **aside** tag:

```
<aside>
    <h2>More Posts</h2>
    <h3>Archives</h3>

    ( CODE OMITTED TO SAVE SPACE )

    <h3>A Word from Some Sponsors</h3>
    <ul>
        <li>PETA</li>
        <li>ASPCA</li>
    </ul>
</aside>
```

5. The last paragraph contains copyright content. It's a perfect footer. Wrap the **footer** tag around the final paragraph, as shown below:

```
<footer>
    <p>© fish-and-fowl.org - all rights reserved - all wrongs reversed</p>
</footer>
```

6. Save the file.

The Section Element

The **section** element is used to divide content into different subject areas. Let's use the tag to group together the **two** articles about birds (one is about **peacocks** and the other's about **eagles**).

1. Wrap the following content in a **section** tag, as shown below:

```
<section>
    <article>
        <h2>Have You Ever Met a Peacock?</h2>
        <h3>It's the Male Who's All Dolled up</h3>
        <p>Peafowl are two Asiatic and one African species...
        <p>Source: <a href="http://en.wikipedia.org..."</p>
    </article>

    <article>
        <h2>The Majestic Eagles Have Landed</h2>
        <h3>Eagle Watching on the Mississippi River</h3>
        <p>Eagles' eyes are extremely powerful, having up to...
        <p>Source: <a href="http://en.wikipedia.org..."</p>
    </article>
</section>
```

2. Let's give the section a logical heading. Directly after the opening **section** tag add the following bold code:

```
<section>
    <h2>Birds</h2>
    <article>
        <h2>Have You Ever Met a Peacock?</h2>
```

3. Wrap the last article (the one about sharks) in a **section** tag.

```
<section>
    <article>
        <h2>Swimming With Sharks</h2>
        <h3>The Whale Shark: The Largest of All Fish</h3>
        <p>The whale shark holds many records for sheer size...
        <p>Source: <a href="http://en.wikipedia.org..."</p>
    </article>
</section>
```

4. Let's give this section a logical heading too. After the section opening tag type:

```
<section>
    <h2>Fish</h2>
    <article>
        <h2>Swimming With Sharks</h2>
```

5. Save the file.

Section vs. Article

An **article** is perfect for syndication: it describes a discrete piece of content that can stand on its own and be reused elsewhere. Think of a blog post or a news story.

A **section** is used to divide content into different subject areas. You are handily grouping articles into sections here but, if you had longer articles, you could, additionally, have sections nested in articles to further divide the content logically.

An Improved Outline

1. In a browser, go back to gsnedders.html5.org/outliner

2. Under **Input HTML**, click the **Browse** or **Choose File** button.

3. Navigate to **Class Files > yourname–HTML5 CSS3 Class > Structural Semantics**.

4. Double–click **semantic-elements.html** to choose it.

5. Click the **Outline this!** button just below the file. You'll notice that the logical structure of the page has been vastly improved with the new sections we just added.

Previous Version

```
1. Fish and Fowl
    1. The Amazing Animal Blog
    2. Navigation
    3. Have You Ever Met a Peacock?
        1. It's the Male Who's All Dolled Up
    4. The Majestic Eagles Have Landed
        1. Eagle Watching on the Mississippi River
    5. Swimming with Sharks
        1. The Whale Shark: The Largest of All Fish
    6. More Posts
        1. Archives
        2. What's on Our Radar
        3. A Word from Some Sponsors
```

New Version

```
1. Fish and Fowl
    1. The Amazing Animal Blog
    2. Navigation
    3. Birds
        1. Have You Ever Met a Peacock?
            1. It's the Male Who's All Dolled Up
        2. The Majestic Eagles Have Landed
            1. Eagle Watching on the Mississippi River
    4. Fish
        1. Swimming with Sharks
            1. The Whale Shark: The Largest of All Fish
    5. More Posts
        1. Archives
        2. What's on Our Radar
        3. A Word from Some Sponsors
```

6. Had we not used HTML semantic tags to partition the content logically, our outline would look a bit confusing:

Has HTML5 Semantic Tags

```
1. Fish and Fowl
    1. The Amazing Animal Blog
    2. Navigation
    3. Birds
        1. Have You Ever Met a Peacock?
            1. It's the Male Who's All Dolled Up
        2. The Majestic Eagles Have Landed
            1. Eagle Watching on the Mississippi River
    4. Fish
        1. Swimming with Sharks
            1. The Whale Shark: The Largest of All Fish
    5. More Posts
        1. Archives
        2. What's on Our Radar
        3. A Word from Some Sponsors
```

No HTML5 Semantic Tags

```
1. Fish and Fowl
    1. The Amazing Animal Blog
    2. Navigation
    3. Birds
    4. Have You Ever Met a Peacock?
        1. It's the Male Who's All Dolled Up
    5. The Majestic Eagles Have Landed
        1. Eagle Watching on the Mississippi River
    6. Fish
    7. Swimming with Sharks
        1. The Whale Shark: The Largest of All Fish
    8. More Posts
        1. Archives
        2. What's on Our Radar
        3. A Word from Some Sponsors
```

The Main Element

Let's define the most important content in the document with the **main** tag. This element will not have any bearing on the document outline but it will add semantic value to the markup. The **main** element's primary purpose is to improve accessibility; it will help screen readers and other assistive technologies understand where the main content begins.

1. Return to **semantic-elements.html** in your code editor.

2. Wrap the two section elements in the **main** tag, as shown below.

```
<main>
    <section>
        <h2>Birds</h2>
        <article>
            <h2>Have You Ever Met a Peacock?</h2>
            ( CODE OMITTED TO SAVE SPACE )

        </article>

        <article>
            <h2>The Majestic Eagles Have Landed</h2>
            ( CODE OMITTED TO SAVE SPACE )

        </article>
    </section>

    <section>
        <h2>Fish</h2>
        <article>
            <h2>Swimming with Sharks</h2>
            ( CODE OMITTED TO SAVE SPACE )

        </article>
    </section>
</main>
```

3. Because this element is relatively new and, as yet, not fully supported across assistive technologies, it's strongly recommended that you use the WAI-ARIA (Web Accessibility Initiative - Accessible Rich Internet Applications) landmark **role** attribute as well, which is more widely supported than is the main element at this time. Add the following attribute to the main tag, around line 22, as follows:

```
<main role="main">
```

NOTE: The **main** element can only be used once per document and it must not be nested inside of an article, aside, footer, header, or nav element.

4. Save the file.

Figure & Figcaption

Let's jazz up the page with an image of an exotic animal.

1. Between the nav and the main content, add some space and around line 22, add the following **img** to the code:

```
</nav>

<img src="img/tawny-frogmouth.jpg" height="346" width="700" alt="Tawny
Frogmouth">

<main role="main">
```

2. Save the file and preview **semantic-elements.html** in a web browser.

   What a cool bird! It would be nice to add a caption to the image to provide details about the bird. Luckily, HTML5 introduced the **figure** element to use in combination with **figcaption** as a semantic way to include an image, chart, or code example accompanied by an explanatory caption. Let's see how it works.

3. Return to **semantic-elements.html** in your code editor.

4. Wrap the **img** tag in the following **figure** element:

```
<figure>
   <img src="img/tawny-frogmouth.jpg" height="346" width="700" alt="Tawny
Frogmouth">
</figure>
```

5. Add the **figcaption** element inside the **figure** tag below the image, as follows:

```
<figure>
   <img src="img/tawny-frogmouth.jpg" height="346" width="700" alt="Tawny
Frogmouth">
   <figcaption></figcaption>
</figure>
```

6. To save you some time, we've provided you with the caption content. Hit **Cmd–O** (Mac) or **Ctrl–O** (Windows) to open a file.

7. Navigate to **Class Files > yourname-Web Dev Class > Structural Semantics > snippets** and open **content-figcaption.html**.

8. Select all the text.

9. Copy it.

10. Close the file and return to **semantic-elements.html**.

11. Paste the code inside the empty **`<figcaption></figcaption>`** tags, as follows:

```
<figcaption>The Tawny Frogmouth (Podargus strigoides) is a type of bird found
throughout the Australian mainland, Tasmania...frogmouths are more closely
related to nightjars and oilbirds. Source: <a href="http://en.wikipedia.org/
wiki/Tawny_frogmouth">Wikipedia</a></figcaption>
```

12. Save the file and preview **semantic-elements.html** in a web browser. Interesting!

    Note the default margin that is added on the left of the figure element. There's a default margin on the right as well, but it's not obvious at this point. In any case, the margins can always be modified later with CSS, if necessary. For now, let's validate the code we have so far to make sure it's sound.

To Validate or Not to Validate

Validation is best used as a tool—a method of quality assurance to test for unclosed HTML elements, typos, and the like—rather than as a goal in and of itself, as there may be times where you need to use non-standard, or non-compliant code, particularly in more forward-thinking websites.

Let's use an online validation tool that was created by Henri Sivonen, a developer at Mozilla. It's validation engine helps drive the validator that the W3C is currently using.

1. Open a browser and go to: html5.validator.nu

2. Under **Validator Input**, go into the menu (which currently says **Address**) and choose **File Upload**.

3. Click the **Browse** or **Choose File** button.

4. Navigate to **Class Files > yourname-HTML5 CSS3 Class > Structural Semantics**.

5. Double–click on **semantic-elements.html**.

6. Click the **Validate** button.

7. Despite a warning about **main** not needing a **role**, the document should be valid HTML5.

    What about the warning? As we mentioned earlier, the **main** element is newer than **role="main"**. While the validator is correct that **role** is redundant, it's recommended to use it until all browsers and screen readers properly implement the **main** element.

Exercise Preview

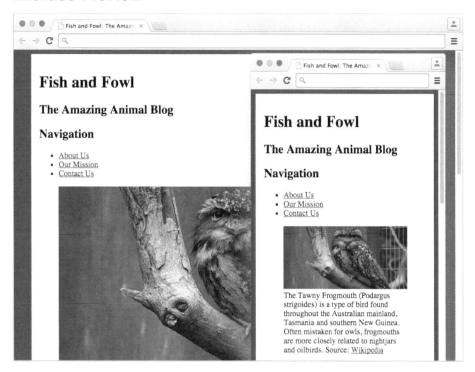

Exercise Overview

In the previous exercise, we learned how to use HTML5 semantic tags to partition our content into logical sections. In this exercise, we'll investigate how the `<div>` tag can and should still be used to group and style content non-semantically. We'll also start to think about how to make our layouts fluid, so they adapt to different-sized browser windows.

1. If you completed the previous exercise, **semantic-elements.html** should still be open in your code editor, and you can skip the following sidebar. If you closed **semantic-elements.html**, re-open it now (from the **Structural Semantics** folder). We recommend you finish the previous exercise (2D) before starting this one. If you haven't finished it, do the following sidebar.

If You Did Not Do the Previous Exercise (2D)

1. Close any files you may have open.

2. In your code editor, open **semantic-elements-with-sections.html** from the **Structural Semantics** folder.

3. Do a **File > Save As** and save the file as **semantic-elements.html**, replacing the older version in your folder.

3A Fluid Layout & Max-Width

Fluid Images

1. Preview **semantic-elements.html** in a browser and take a moment to click and drag the edge of the browser window in and out to resize the window, making sure to make it fairly wide and then narrow at some point. Notice how the text-based content is fluid—it reflows to the edge of the window. The image, on the other hand, maintains its width. Let's make this image resize to fit the window.

2. Return to your code editor.

3. Add a **<style>** tag to the head of the document as follows:

```
<!DOCTYPE html>
<html lang="en">
<head>
    <meta charset="UTF-8">
    <title>Fish and Fowl: The Amazing Animal Blog</title>
    <style>
    </style>
</head>
```

4. Add the following new rule for the **img** element:

```
<style>
    img {
        width: 100%;
    }
</style>
```

5. Save the file and preview it in a browser.

6. Drag the edge of the browser window in and out to resize the window. Wow, the image doesn't look good because it is getting stretched. The width is changing, but not the height. We need to maintain the image's aspect ratio so it looks normal.

7. Return to your code editor.

8. Down in the page, find the **img** tag and delete its **height** and **width** attributes, so you end up with the following code:

```
<img src="img/tawny-frogmouth.jpg" alt="Tawny Frogmouth">
```

9. Save the file and preview it in a browser.

10. Resize the window again. This is an improvement. But, still, when the window is quite wide, the image is huge and it's not really optimized to be quite so large. It would be much better if the image could not be scaled beyond its original width. Luckily, there's a CSS property we can use that will do the trick: **max-width**.

11. Return to your code editor.

12. Change the **img** rule's **width** to **max-width** as shown below:

```
img {
    max-width: 100%;
}
```

NOTE: Max-width is short for maximum width. This ensures images will be 100% of the width of its parent container or less (because it will not scale images up beyond their native width).

13. Save the file and preview it in a browser, making sure to test out how the image scales in the browser window. Perfect! Now let's improve the layout of the rest of the content.

Limiting Content with Max-Width

Although the text-based content in the page is already fluid by default—because each semantic section of the page is 100% of the browser's width and the text simply wraps inside the sections—the legibility of the content can be improved. We can start by keeping the fluidity of the page but limiting the content area. Once again, **max-width** will come in handy.

1. Return to your code editor.

2. In the styles at the top of the document, add the following new rule just above the rule for **img**, like so:

```
body {
    max-width: 800px;
}
img {
    max-width: 100%;
}
```

3. Save the file and preview it in a browser. So far, so good. If you resize the window, you'll notice that the content is nice and fluid when the window is on the narrower side and, when the window is wider, the content does not extend beyond 800 pixels.

   This page would be a bit nicer to look at if the content were centered in the window, though. Let's do that next.

4. Return to your code editor.

5. Edit the rule for **body** to create automatic margins on the left and the right of the content, as follows:

```
body {
    max-width: 800px;
    margin-left: auto;
    margin-right: auto;
}
```

6. Save the file and preview it in a browser. It looks great at a wider width but at the more narrow sizes, the content is a bit close to the edge. Let's set a width for the content after all. We can keep things fluid while making sure that there's more breathing room between the content and the edge of the browser.

7. Return to your code editor.

8. Edit the rule for **body** like so:

```
body {
    width: 90%;
    max-width: 800px;
    margin-left: auto;
    margin-right: auto;
}
```

9. Save the file and preview it in a browser. Nice! At a narrow browser width, the content is now much more legible.

Creating a Wrapper & Using ID Selectors

The page layout is shaping up, but if we wanted to create separate background colors for the page and the content (as we did in an earlier exercise), we really don't have the proper markup in the document to accommodate this. Instead of using the <body> as our main container for the content, let's create a wrapper.

So far, we have used HTML5 semantic tags to partition our content into logical sections. Now we'd like to group the content together in order to style it. When you're making a decision about wrapping content in an element purely because you want to style it, the <div> tag can and should still be used. Let's wrap all the content in a <div>.

1. Return to your code editor.

2. To wrap a div tag around all the content of the document, type the following opening tag (highlighted in bold) just below the opening **body** tag.

```
<body>
    <div>
    <header>
        <h1>Fish and Fowl</h1>
```

3. Close the tag just above the **closing body** tag (near the bottom of the code), as shown below:

```
        <footer>
            <p>© fish-and-fowl.org - all rights reserved - all wrongs reversed</p>
        </footer>
    </div>
</body>
</html>
```

In more complex layouts, we're bound to have more than just one <div>. Although that's not the case here, as a best practice, let's add an ID to the <div> to style it more specifically.

4. Add the following ID to your opening <div> tag, as follows:

```
<body>
    <div id="wrapper">
    <header>
        <h1>Fish and Fowl</h1>
```

The ID you just typed will allow you to give this div its own unique, individual style based on an **ID selector**. Spaces and special characters must be avoided in ID names, just as you must avoid them in class selector names. Unlike class selectors, however, no two elements on a page may use the same ID.

5. Change the rule for **body** so it's now a rule for **#wrapper**, like so:

```
#wrapper {
    width: 90%;
    max-width: 800px;
    margin-left: auto;
    margin-right: auto;
}
```

When writing an ID selector, you use the number sign, or **hash mark** (#) prior to the name of the selector. This alerts the browser to the fact that it must select and style the element with the corresponding ID. Remember: no two elements may share the same ID. This makes an ID selector the most specific type of selector.

6. Let's also set the background-color for #wrapper, as follows:

```
#wrapper {
   width: 90%;
   max-width: 800px;
   margin-left: auto;
   margin-right: auto;
   background-color: #fff;
}
```

Hexadecimal Shorthand

CSS color hex values can be fully written out or abbreviated with shorthand. When the value consists of **3 identical pairs**, it can be written as a 3-digit shorthand **#fff** (instead of the full 6-digit **#ffffff** value).

This shorthand can only be used for any color that has **3 identical pairs** of characters. So instead of **#33cc66** you could just write **#3c6**. Colors such as **#0075a4** cannot be shortened. Going forward, we'll use shorthand hex values wherever possible.

7. Now let's add a new rule for **body** in order to make the background of the page darker. Add the following new rule just above the rule for **#wrapper**:

```
body {
   background-color: #555;
}
#wrapper {
   width: 90%;
   max-width: 800px;
   margin-left: auto;
   margin-right: auto;
   background-color: #fff;
}
```

8. Save the file and preview it in a browser. The content now pops quite a bit but could use more padding, for certain.

9. Return to your code editor.

10. Add the following property declaration to the rule for #wrapper:

```
#wrapper {
    width: 90%;
    max-width: 800px;
    margin-left: auto;
    margin-right: auto;
    background-color: #fff;
    padding: 16px;
}
```

11. While we're here, let's reorganize the styles so the tag selectors (least specific) are above the ID selector (more specific). Move the img rule so it sits below the rule for body. Your finished styles should look as follows:

```
<style>
    body {
        background-color: #555;
    }
    img {
        max-width: 100%;
    }
    #wrapper {
        width: 90%;
        max-width: 800px;
        margin-right: auto;
        margin-left: auto;
        background-color: #fff;
        padding: 16px;
    }
</style>
```

12. Save the file and preview it in a browser. Much improved! This page could use a bit more style, but we're finished for now with regard to creating a fluid layout. If you finish early, feel free to experiment with styling the content a bit more.

Revolution Travel: Real-World Layout

Exercise Preview

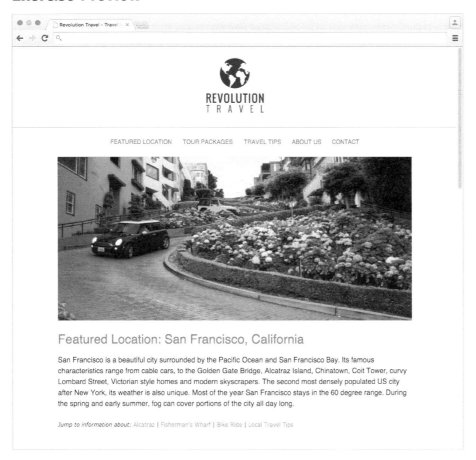

Exercise Overview

This is the first in a series of exercises in which you'll lay out a complete website. In this exercise, we'll begin by laying out the basics of a single page. We'll build the structure of the page and place content inside each section.

Getting Started

1. We'll be using a new folder of provided files for this exercise. This website folder contains images, some partially made webpages for you to finish, and a couple of code snippets, one of which contains tagged HTML content for you to copy and paste. Close any files you may have open in your code editor to avoid confusion.

2. We'll be working with files in a folder named **Revolution Travel** located in **Class Files > yourname-Web Dev Class**.

   TIP: It's often beneficial to see your entire website folder as you work. Many code editors allow you to do so. If you are working in Sublime Text, for instance, you can go to **File > Open** (Mac) or **File > Open Folder** (Windows), navigate to **Class Files > yourname-Web Dev Class > Revolution Travel** and hit **Open** (Mac) or **Select Folder** (Windows).

3. In your code editor, open **sanfran.html** from the **Revolution Travel** folder.

4. **Title** the document by editing the code as follows:

```
<!DOCTYPE html>
<html lang="en">
<head>
    <meta charset="UTF-8">
    <title>Revolution Travel - Travel Info for San Francisco, CA</title>
</head>
<body>

</body>
</html>
```

5. Save the file.

Coding Up the Sections

1. To see a finished version of the page you'll be building, navigate to the **Desktop** and go into the **Class Files** folder, then **yourname-Web Dev Class** folder, then **Revolution Travel Done**.

2. **Ctrl–click** (Mac) or **Right–click** (Windows) on **sanfran.html**, go to **Open with** and select your favorite browser.

3. Notice that the page is composed of four main sections: a header, navigation, main content, and a footer on the bottom. (The footer is subtle, as it only contains the copyright information.) Let's code up each of these sections.

4. Return to **sanfran.html** in your code editor.

5. Add the following sectioning tags (highlighted in bold) inside the **body** tag:

```
<body>
    <header></header>
    <nav></nav>
    <main role="main"></main>
    <footer></footer>
</body>
```

6. If you were to preview the file in a browser, you wouldn't see a thing. By default, section elements have no border, no background, and are only as tall as the content inside of them. Browsers will render these sections as block-level elements.

> **Block-level Elements**
>
> **Block-level** elements stack on top of one another like a child's building blocks. Each one begins on a new line and takes up 100% of the width of their parent containers. Although "block-level" is not technically defined for sectioning elements that are new in HTML5, most browsers will render these elements according to the block-level formatting model. Paragraphs, headings, divs, and lists are some other block-level elements that we've already covered.

Adding Content to the Header

1. The **header** should feature the company's logo. Add the following bold code:

```
<body>
    <header><img src="images/revolution-logo.png"></header>
    <nav></nav>
    <main role="main"></main>
    <footer></footer>
</body>
```

2. While you're here, don't forget to add the alt text:

```
<img src="images/revolution-logo.png" alt="Revolution Travel">
```

3. Save the file.

4. Preview the page in a browser to see the header image.

Adding the Main Content

1. To save you some time, we've tagged up most of the main content for the page and saved it into a file. In a code editor, open **main-content.html** from the **snippets** folder (in the **Revolution Travel** folder).

2. Select all the code (**Cmd–A** (Mac) or **Ctrl–A** (Windows)).

3. Copy it (**Cmd–C** (Mac) or **Ctrl–C** (Windows)).

4. Close the file.

5. You should be back in **sanfran.html**.

6. Place the cursor between the **<main>** opening and closing tags.

7. To make our code more legible, hit **Return** (Mac) or **Enter** (Windows) to place the closing </main> tag on its own line like so:

   ```
   <main role="main">

   </main>
   ```

8. Paste (**Cmd–V** (Mac) or **Ctrl–V** (Windows)) the code into the **main** section. If you're using Sublime Text, press **Cmd–Shift–V** (Mac) or **Ctrl–Shift–V** (Windows) to paste the code so it matches the current indention level.

9. Save the file.

Adding the Nav Content

The first five lines of the content you just pasted into the main section should actually form the content of the navigation. Let's move them into their appropriate section.

1. Place your cursor between the **<nav>** opening and closing tags and hit **Return** (Mac) or **Enter** (Windows) to place the closing tag on its own line like so:

   ```
   <nav>

   </nav>
   ```

2. In the **main** section, select the first five lines, starting with **Featured Location** and ending with **Contact**.

3. Cut the text (**Cmd–X** (Mac) or **Ctrl–X** (Windows)).

4. Now paste it into the **nav** like so:

   ```
   <nav>
       Featured Location
       Tour Packages
       Travel Tips
       About Us
       Contact
   </nav>
   ```

5. To clean up the code to be a bit more legible, take a moment to delete any **whitespace** (empty lines) that remains in the **main** section.

6. Let's also mark up the nav element with the additional semantic value of an unordered list. Edit the **nav** contents to wrap a `<ul>` tag around all the content as well as an `<li>` tag around each nav item, as follows:

```
<nav>
   <ul>
      <li>Featured Location</li>
      <li>Tour Packages</li>
      <li>Travel Tips</li>
      <li>About Us</li>
      <li>Contact</li>
   </ul>
</nav>
```

7. Save the file.

Adding the Footer Content

1. Scroll down to the code at the bottom of the page. Place your cursor between the **<footer>** opening and closing tags and hit **Return** (Mac) or **Enter** (Windows) to place the closing tag on its own line like so:

```
<footer>

</footer>
```

2. Select the last paragraph of the main content—the copyright paragraph—and cut it (**Cmd–X** (Mac) or **Ctrl–X** (Windows)).

3. Paste it into the **footer** like so:

```
<footer>
   <p>© Revolution Travel</p>
</footer>
```

4. Take a moment to delete any whitespace that remains in the **main** section to clean up the code a bit.

5. Save the file.

6. Return to the browser, and reload the page to see your content. Nothing has been styled yet, so the content just stacks in a logical order and wraps to the edge of the browser window.

Marking Up the Headings

Let's mark up the text a bit to give more structure to the topics on the page.

Revolution Travel: Real-World Layout

1. Return to your code, scroll to the top of the page, and find the first paragraph in the **main** section.

2. As shown below, edit the code to change the p tags to **h1** tags:

```
<main role="main">
    <h1>Featured Location: San Francisco, California</h1>
```

3. As shown below, edit the code (a few lines down) to change the p tags to **h2** tags:

```
<h2>Things to Do</h2>
<p>San Francisco is filled with culture, fine eating, nightlife and more. From
beaches and parks, museums, bike riding, cable cars, to street performers,
there is always something to do. The hard part is deciding how you'll spend
your time! Here are a few recommendations:</p>
```

4. A little below that edit the **Local Travel Tips** paragraph to make it a heading level 2, like so:

```
<h2>Local Travel Tips</h2>
<p>San Francisco has pretty mild temperatures all year long. While that means
you won't be too freezing or too hot, don't be fooled by the lore of "sunny
California." San Fran does tend to be on the chilly side, especially at night
or when the wind gets blowing. Bring some extra layers in case you need them.
Most people are surprised to find it's colder than they expected.</p>
```

5. Save the file.

6. Return to the browser and reload the page to see your improved markup.

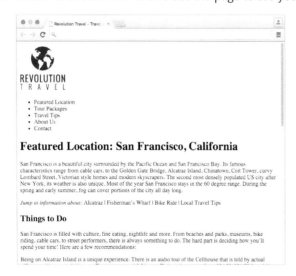

7. At this point the page doesn't have much going on but you now have most of the HTML structure needed to start styling the elements. You can keep **sanfran.html** open in the browser and the code editor. You'll continue with this file in the next exercise.

How to Create a Brand New HTML File

You started this exercise with a provided HTML file to streamline the flow of the exercise. In the real world, you may want to create a file from scratch. Here's how to quickly create a new HTML document in either Sublime Text or Dreamweaver.

In Sublime Text (with Emmet installed):

1. Go to **File > New File**.

2. Save the file as **some-file-name.html**

3. To quickly create all the basic HTML tags, type an **exclamation point** (!) and hit **Tab**.

In Dreamweaver:

1. Go to **File > New**.

2. Select **New Document** (used to be **Blank Page**) then the following:

   Document Type: **HTML**

   Framework: **None**

   Doc Type: **HTML 5**

3. Hit **Create**.

The Box Model

Exercise Preview

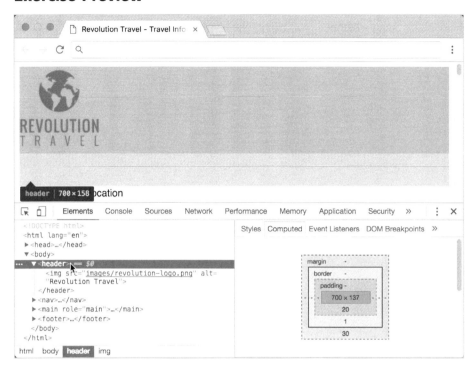

Exercise Overview

All HTML elements can hold content and have empty space both inside and outside of them, so it is very helpful to consider them as boxes when thinking about styling these elements with CSS. In this exercise, we'll explore this CSS Box Model to see how the width, padding, and margin properties can allow us to control the page layout.

1. If you completed the previous exercise, **sanfran.html** should still be open, and you can skip the following sidebar. If you closed **sanfran.html**, re-open it now. We recommend you finish the previous exercise (3B) before starting this one. If you haven't finished it, do the following sidebar.

> **If You Did Not Do the Previous Exercise (3B)**
>
> 1. Close any files you may have open.
>
> 2. On the **Desktop**, go to **Class Files > yourname-Web Dev Class**.
>
> 3. Delete the **Revolution Travel** folder if it exists.
>
> 4. Duplicate the **Revolution Travel Ready for Box Model** folder.
>
> 5. Rename the folder to **Revolution Travel**.

3C The Box Model

Getting Started

1. In **sanfran.html**, add a **<style>** tag to the head of the document as follows:

```
<!DOCTYPE html>
<html lang="en">
<head>
   <meta charset="UTF-8">
   <title>Revolution Travel - Travel Info for San Francisco, CA</title>
   <style>
   </style>
</head>
```

2. Save the file.

Setting Width & Display Properties

The header and nav content of this page stretch across 100% of the browser window in our design, but the main content and footer should be slightly more narrow. Let's set a size for the main content so its content doesn't stretch across the entire page.

1. In **sanfran.html** add the following code (highlighted in bold) inside the **style** tag in the head section:

```
<style>
   main {
      width: 90%;
   }
</style>
```

Let's make the **footer** the same width as the **main** content.

2. Add the following new rule (highlighted in bold) below the **main** rule in the style tag.

```
   main {
      width: 90%;
   }
   footer {
      width: 90%;
   }
</style>
```

NOTE: Height is usually not specified, as the content may be continually edited and, ideally, an element's height should be left to the default **auto** to accommodate these changes.

3. Save the file.

4. Preview the file in a browser. The main content is now a bit more narrow than it was. Although it's not noticeable because of the sparse content in the footer, setting the width to match the main content will certainly come in handy later, should we need to add more content to the footer.

   TIP: Keep this file open in the browser so you can simply reload the page to test the code as you work.

The Box Model

Specifying an element's width, as you've done for both the main and footer sections, is just about the simplest way you can describe an HTML element's "box," or how much space it takes up in the flow of the document.

Any element can be considered a box—not just section elements and divs. The box model allows you to not only specify the **width** and **height** of content, it allows you to place **padding** within the element's box and **margins** between the element and other content on the page. You will explore padding, margin, and the **border** property—which is also part of the box model—later in this exercise.

---

5. If possible, preview **sanfran.html** in **Internet Explorer**.

   You will notice that the width of the main element has not changed. This is because, even though the **main** element has been in the HTML5 specification since late 2012, Internet Explorer (IE) does not recognize this element and treats it as a new, unspecified element.

   When elements are unspecified, browsers display them as inline elements. Sadly, inline elements do not accept a width property. We need to give IE a hand here and let it know to display **main** as a block element, so we can style it accordingly.

6. Return to your code editor.

7. Edit the rule for **main** to add the display property, as follows:

```
main {
    width: 90%;
    display: block;
}
```

8. Save the file.

9. If possible, preview **sanfran.html** in **Internet Explorer** once more. The main element is now responding to our rule. Excellent!

Inline vs. Block-level

Block-level elements stack on top of one another like a child's building blocks. Paragraphs, headings, section elements, divs, and lists are some common block-level elements that we use on a regular basis.

Inline elements are rendered next to one another in a row. Anchors (links), images, and the <span> element are some of the inline elements we've used so far in class.

The difference goes a bit further. Essentially, manipulating the box-model is more limited for inline elements. While block-level elements can be controlled by changing the width, height, padding, margin, and border of the element, inline elements are only as wide as their content. They do not respond to CSS changes to their width or height. Margin and padding are also handled differently: margin and padding will only work horizontally on inline elements (padding on the top and bottom of inline elements will, technically, be present but often bleed into other lines above and below these elements).

Limiting Content with Max-Width

1. While still previewing sanfran.html in any browser, take a moment to see how wide the main content can get when the browser is maximized. At a certain point, the content becomes illegible. Max-width will allow us to limit the content to a width that is more reader-friendly.

2. Return to your code editor.

3. Edit the rule for **main** to add the following new property declaration:

```
main {
    width: 90%;
    max-width: 800px;
    display: block;
}
```

4. The width of the footer content should also be limited to 800 pixels, should the content ever be edited beyond what's currently there. Add the following property to the rule for **footer** as well:

```
footer {
    width: 90%;
    max-width: 800px;
}
```

5. Save the file and preview your change in the browser. As in a previous exercise, we see that max-width allows you to both have a fluid layout but limit the content when necessary.

Styling the Text

The text-based content needs to be styled so it's more legible and attractive. We'll start by creating a rule for the body tag. By setting text defaults in the parent tag (the body tag), all the text-based children of this element will inherit the style properties.

1. Back in your code editor, add the following code (highlighted in bold) inside the style tag above the **main** rule:

```
body {
    font-family: sans-serif;
    font-size: 16px;
    line-height: 24px;
}
main {
    width: 90%;
    max-width: 800px;
    display: block;
}
```

NOTE: Setting the font-family to sans-serif typically gets you the best results cross-platform. Most Macs will default to Helvetica and most Windows users will see Arial as a default. There may be cases where users have set their default sans-serif font to something off the beaten path. In these cases, that is the font they'll see. If this is unacceptable to you for some reason, you could use a more specific font-stack like Helvetica, Arial, sans-serif, for instance.

2. Save the file, return to the browser, and reload the page. Nicely done.

3. Take note of how the headings are automatically sized proportionally to the default text size of the body element. Wonderful!

Let's set a custom font-size for headings and add a little stylistic flair while we're at it. We'll start with heading level 1.

3C

3C The Box Model

4. Return to your code editor.

5. Add the following new rule (in bold) below the **body** rule:

```
body {
    font-family: sans-serif;
    font-size: 16px;
    line-height: 24px;
}
h1 {
    font-size: 28px;
    color: #6a8e6b;
}
```

6. Save the file, return to the browser, and reload the page to see your heading style. Great! Take a moment, though, to pull the browser window in so the page is narrow and the heading wraps. The line-height we declared as the default for the **body** rule looks appropriate for the paragraphs but is too tight for the significantly larger font-size of the h1. Let's modify this.

7. Return to your code editor.

8. Add the following new property declaration to your rule for **h1**:

```
h1 {
    font-size: 28px;
    color: #6a8e6b;
    line-height: 30px;
}
```

While we're here, for a nice consistent design, let's make our heading level 2 elements look the same but with a smaller font-size.

6. Add the following new rule for **h2** (in bold) below the **h1** rule like so:

```
h1 {
    font-size: 28px;
    color: #6a8e6b;
    line-height: 30px;
}
h2 {
    font-size: 18px;
    color: #6a8e6b;
}
```

7. Save the file, return to the browser, and reload the page to see your stylin' headings.

The Margin Property

Let's add some sorely needed space between the different sections of the page. Margin comes in handy for placing space between elements. Margin is always placed **outside** an element's "box."

1. Return to **sanfran.html** in your code editor.

2. Let's start by putting more space between the header and the navigation. We can add **margin** below the header. Above the **main** rule, add the following new rule:

```
header {
    margin-bottom: 30px;
}
main {
    width: 90%;
    max-width: 800px;
    display: block;
}
```

3. Save the file, return to the browser, and reload the page to see that there is now more space below the header. We could use some more space between the navigation and the main content as well.

4. Return to your code editor.

5. Above the **main** rule, add the following new rule:

```
nav {
    margin-bottom: 30px;
}
main {
    width: 90%;
    max-width: 800px;
    display: block;
}
```

6. While you're here, add a margin declaration to the **main** rule as well:

```
main {
    width: 90%;
    max-width: 800px;
    display: block;
    margin-bottom: 30px;
}
```

7. Save the file, return to the browser, and reload the page to see the improved spacing.

   While you're reviewing the page, notice that, while the paragraphs in this page have a nice line-height, we could use more space between each paragraph. To do that we will need to modify the **margin** property. This is similar to space after or before a paragraph in other page layout applications.

8. Return to your code editor and add the following new rule (in bold) below the **h2** rule like so:

```
h2 {
    font-size: 18px;
    color: #6a8e6b;
}
p {
    margin-bottom: 22px;
}
```

9. Save the file, return to the browser, and reload the page to see a subtle change in the space between paragraphs.

The Padding & Border Properties

Padding is always placed **inside** an element's "box"—it adds visual width and height to the element.

1. Return to your code editor.

2. Let's create more of a visual separation between the header and the nav with a CSS border. Add the following new property to the rule for **header**:

```
header {
    margin-bottom: 30px;
    border-bottom: 1px solid #4a5f04;
}
```

3. Save the file, return to the browser, and reload the page to see the border. It looks decent but there should be a bit more space between the logo and the border. This is where padding comes in handy.

4. Return to your code editor.

5. Add the following new property to the rule for **header**:

```
header {
    margin-bottom: 30px;
    border-bottom: 1px solid #4a5f04;
    padding-bottom: 20px;
}
```

6. Save the file, return to the browser, and reload the page to see the improved spacing between the logo and the border.

7. You can keep **sanfran.html** open in the browser and the code editor. You'll continue with this file in the next exercise.

Margin vs. Padding

The margin and padding properties can be used to fine-tune the space between elements in a layout, though each adds space a bit differently. When thinking of a box, **padding** is **inside** the box. Padding actually opens up an element's box by making it appear wider and/or taller. For instance, if the element has a background color or border, the padding stretches the background and pushes the border farther away from the content.

Margin, on the other hand, is **outside** the element's box. The space is transparent.

For more information and to see a graphic that illustrates the difference between these two properties, see the **Box Model** reference at the back of the workbook.

Floats & Images

Exercise Preview

Things to Do

San Francisco is filled with culture, fine eating, nightlife and more. From beaches and parks, museums, bike riding, cable cars, to street performers, there is always something to do. The hard part is deciding how you'll spend your time! Here are a few recommendations:

Being on Alcatraz Island is a unique experience. There is an audio tour of the Cellhouse that is told by actual officers and inmates of Alcatraz. Tours run around 2.5 hours. Ticket prices range from $24.50-$31.50 for adults and $15.25-$18.75 for children (5–11). Toddlers (0–4) are free. The tour leaves from Pier 33 and is easily accessible by public transportation. After the tour, why not grab a bite to eat or do some shopping at Fisherman's Wharf? Back to Top

Fisherman's Wharf is one of San Francisco's most popular destinations because there is so much to see and do. You can catch a bay cruise to Alcatraz or the Golden Gate Bridge. Ride a cable car, rent a bike, tour the aquarium and more. There are shops, boats, shows, and even sea lions to watch! One of the main attractions though is the seafood. From sidewalk vendors selling shrimp or crab sandwiches to fine dining establishments, the seafood lover will find something fresh and delicious to eat. Back to Top

For a great outdoor activity that involves exercise, rent a bike! It is the best way to quickly see many of San Francisco's landmarks. Blazing Saddles has several locations to rent a bike. They provide maps of popular bikes routes and destinations. Bike across the Golden Gate Bridge, see the giant Redwoods, tour charming Sausalito, and catch a ferry ride back. Back to Top

Exercise Overview

The page is coming together, but it could use some more images. In this exercise, we'll add some images and also learn how to position images alongside text by using the float property. Additionally, we'll review the usefulness of the class selector.

1. If you completed the previous exercise, **sanfran.html** should still be open, and you can skip the following sidebar. If you closed **sanfran.html**, re-open it now. We recommend you finish the previous exercises (3B–3C) before starting this one. If you haven't finished them, do the following sidebar.

If You Did Not Do the Previous Exercises (3B–3C)

1. Close any files you may have open.

2. On the **Desktop**, go to **Class Files > yourname-Web Dev Class**.

3. Delete the **Revolution Travel** folder if it exists.

4. Duplicate the **Revolution Travel Ready for Floats** folder.

5. Rename the folder to **Revolution Travel**.

3D Floats & Images

Adding a Hero Image

In web design lingo, a hero image is often the first visual a visitor encounters on the site. It is a large banner-style image prominently placed at the top of a webpage and its purpose is to provide a sort of visual overview of the page's content. Let's add a hero image to our page about visiting San Francisco.

1. In **sanfran.html**, add an image inside **main**, above the **h1** tag:

```
<main role="main">
   <img src="images/san-fran-lombard.jpg" alt="San Francisco Landmark: Lombard
Street">
   <h1>Featured Location: San Francisco, California</h1>
```

2. Save the file and preview it in a browser to see your image. Looks good! Resize the window, making sure to make it fairly wide and then narrow at some point. Let's make images resize to fit the window.

3. Return to your code editor.

4. Scroll up to the styles and, below the rule for the **p** tag, add the following new rule for the **img** element:

```
p {
   margin-bottom: 22px;
}
img {
   max-width: 100%;
}
```

Remember that max-width ensures images will be 100% of the width of its parent container or less (because it will not scale images up beyond their native width).

5. Save the file and preview it in a browser, making sure to test out how the image scales down to always fit within the browser window. Perfect!

Adding More Images

1. Return to **sanfran.html** in your code editor.

2. Around line 66, you should see the **h2** for **Things to Do**. We'll add three images to this section of the page.

3. Add the first image just inside the paragraph that begins, **Being on Alcatraz Island**, as follows:

```
<p><img src="images/logo-alcatraz.jpg" alt="Alcatraz Cruises">Being on
Alcatraz Island is a unique experience. ... Back to Top</p>
```

4. Add the second image inside the paragraph that begins, **Fisherman's Wharf**, as follows:

```
<p><img src="images/logo-fishermans-wharf.jpg"
alt="Fisherman's Wharf">Fisherman's Wharf is one of San Francisco's most
popular destinations because there is so much to see and do. ...
Back to Top</p>
```

5. Add the third image inside the paragraph that begins, **For a great outdoor activity**, as follows:

```
<p><img src="images/logo-blazing-saddles.jpg" alt="Blazing Saddles">For a
great outdoor activity that involves exercise, rent a bike! ... Back to Top</p>
```

6. Save the file, return to the browser, and reload the page to see the three images at the beginning of each of these paragraphs. Notice the awkward alignment.

We'd like the images to "float" alongside the text on the left and right, just like we would add text wrap in a print layout. Luckily, the CSS **float** property was designed for just this purpose.

Floating the Images with Class Selectors

1. Return to **sanfran.html** in your code editor.

   If the goal was to float all images on the page to the left of the text (or, for that matter, to the right of the text), we could simply create a new rule for the img tag. Using a tag selector allows us to target all of the same type of element with the same exact style.

   The goal here, however, is to float just a few of the images on the page. What's more, we'd like some to float left and others to float right. Class selectors are the best selector for the job: we can assign them just to specific elements and we can reuse them as many times we need wherever we like on the page.

2. Scroll up to the styles in the code.

3. Right before the closing `</style>` tag, after the rule for **footer**, add the following new rule. (Remember that the dot before **img-left** is there on purpose. That is what makes it a class selector.)

```
    footer {
       width: 90%;
       max-width: 800px;
    }
    .img-left {
       float: left;
    }
</style>
```

4. Now that you created a new rule, you need to assign the class to the images you actually want to float left. Find the image tag for the Alcatraz Cruises logo, and add the following bold class attribute and value:

```
<img src="images/logo-alcatraz.jpg" class="img-left" alt="Alcatraz Cruises">
```

5. Take a moment to check the code for typos. Remember: the value of class is simply **img-left**. You do not type the dot preceding a class name in HTML.

6. Save the file, return to the browser, and reload the page.

7. Scroll down to the **Things to Do** section to see your rule for .img-left in action! Let's add another rule to float the next image to the right.

8. Return to **sanfran.html** in your code editor and scroll up to the styles.

9. Just after the rule for **.img-left**, add the following new rule (in bold):

```
    .img-left {
        float: left;
    }
    .img-right {
        float: right;
    }
</style>
```

10. Now let's assign the class to the image you want to float right. Find the code for the Fisherman's Wharf logo and add the following bold code:

```
<img src="images/logo-fishermans-wharf.jpg" class="img-right" alt="Fisherman's Wharf">
```

11. While you're here in the source code, let's make the third image float left to match the first image. On the Blazing Saddles image, add the following bold code:

```
<img src="images/logo-blazing-saddles.jpg" class="img-left" alt="Blazing Saddles">
```

12. Save the file, return to the browser, and reload the page.

13. Scroll down to see the three images floating nicely beside their paragraphs. The graphics are a little close to the text. As a finishing touch, let's add a margin to improve the spacing.

Adding Margin to the Floated Images

1. Return to **sanfran.html** in your code editor and scroll up to the styles.

2. Edit the rule for **.img-left** by adding the following new property (in bold):

```
.img-left {
    float: left;
    margin-right: 15px;
}
```

3. Now edit the rule for **.img-right** by adding the following new property:

```
.img-right {
    float: right;
    margin-left: 15px;
}
```

4. Save the file, return to the browser, and reload the page to see the improved layout.

5. You can keep **sanfran.html** open in the browser and the code editor. You'll continue with this file in the next exercise.

Exercise Preview

Featured Location: San Francisco, California

San Francisco is a beautiful city surrounded by the Pacific Ocean and San Francisco Bay. Its famous characteristics range from cable cars, to the Golden Gate Bridge, Alcatraz Island, Chinatown, Coit Tower, curvy Lombard Street, Victorian style homes and modern skyscrapers. The second most densely populated US city after New York, its weather is also unique. Most of the year San Francisco stays in the 60 degree range. During the spring and early summer, fog can cover portions of the city all day long.

Jump to information about: Alcatraz | Fisherman's Wharf | Bike Ride | Local Travel Tips

Exercise Overview

This exercise will refresh you on how to link to other pages within your site and how to code external links that open in a new browser tab or window. You will also beef up your linking skills by wrapping links around images and creating link shortcuts to different sections within a single webpage.

1. If you completed the previous exercise, **sanfran.html** should still be open, and you can skip the following sidebar. If you closed **sanfran.html**, re-open it now. We recommend you finish the previous exercises (3B–3D) before starting this one. If you haven't finished them, do the following sidebar.

> **If You Did Not Do the Previous Exercises (3B–3D)**
>
> 1. Close any files you may have open.
>
> 2. On the **Desktop**, go to **Class Files > yourname-Web Dev Class**.
>
> 3. Delete the **Revolution Travel** folder if it exists.
>
> 4. Duplicate the **Revolution Travel Ready for Links** folder.
>
> 5. Rename the folder to **Revolution Travel**.

Coding Links to Pages Within a Site

1. Let's begin by coding the navigation links that lead to other pages on our site. In **sanfran.html**, find the **nav** (just after the start of the **body** tag). Wrap the following anchors and hrefs (in bold) around the text in the nav:

```
<nav>
   <ul>
      <li><a href="sanfran.html">Featured Location</a></li>
      <li><a href="packages.html">Tour Packages</a></li>
      <li><a href="tips.html">Travel Tips</a></li>
      <li><a href="about.html">About Us</a></li>
      <li><a href="contact.html">Contact</a></li>
   </ul>
</nav>
```

TIP: If you are coding in Sublime Text, you can select code and then hit **Ctrl–Shift–W** (Mac) or **Alt–Shift–W** (Windows) to wrap a tag around your selection. If you are using Dreamweaver, you can use **Cmd–T** (Mac) or **Ctrl–T** (Windows) to wrap a tag around a selection.

When linking from one file to another file in a website, you can use **relative links**. The links are relative to the location of the file in which you are coding. If both the file you are in and the one you are linking to are in the same folder (like ours are), all you have to type for the value of the **href** (hyperlink reference) is the file name.

2. Save the file.

3. Preview **sanfran.html** in a browser to test your links. (These pages have been provided for you and are not styled yet. We'll style them in a later exercise.)

4. Hit the **Back** button on the browser to return to **sanfran.html**. Leave this page open in the browser so you can simply reload the page to see your new code as you work.

Wrapping Links Around Images

1. Let's add a link around the logo image. Traditionally, the logo image links to the index, or homepage. Return to **sanfran.html** in your code editor.

2. Just above the **nav**, there's a logo image inside the **header**. Wrap the image in an anchor tag with a hyperlink reference to the index page as shown below in bold:

```
<header><a href="index.html"><img src="images/revolution-logo.png"
alt="Revolution Travel"></a></header>
```

3. Save the file and reload your page in a browser to test out the link. You should be taken to the index page. (This is another unstyled file we have provided for you.)

4. Hit the **Back** button on the browser to return to **sanfran.html**.

5. If you were to preview the page in **Internet Explorer** (**IE**) version 10 or earlier, you would notice that the image has a border around it.

   In older versions of IE, hyperlinked images are highlighted with an unsightly border. Let's get rid of it.

6. Return to **sanfran.html** in your code editor and scroll up to see the styles.

7. Add the following new property to the rule for **img**:

```
img {
    max-width: 100%;
    border: 0;
}
```

8. Save the file and, if possible, preview in Internet Explorer to see that the border has disappeared!

Creating Links to Other Websites

1. Return to **sanfran.html** in your code editor.

2. Scroll down to the **main** section and find the heading that says, **Things to Do**.

   There are three images in this section of the page, each of which needs to be wrapped in an anchor tag with an href to the appropriate external website.

3. Find the image for **Alcatraz Cruises**, and wrap an anchor tag around it as shown below in bold:

```
<p><a href="http://www.alcatrazcruises.com/"><img src="images/logo-
alcatraz.jpg" class="img-left" alt="Alcatraz Cruises"></a>
```

4. Save the file and reload your page in a browser to test out the link. Awesome.

   Linking to another website is as easy as typing the absolute URL to that web address as the value of the href. You must always use **http://** (hypertext transfer protocol) or **https://** (HTTP secure), depending on which protocol the site you are linking to uses. Your best bet is to copy the URL directly from the browser's address bar.

5. Hit the browser's **Back** button to return to **sanfran.html**.

   Wait a minute. There's a better way to make sure a user returns to your website after they follow an external link: the best thing to do is to specify that the URL should open up in a separate browser tab or window.

6. Return to **sanfran.html** in your code editor. Edit your anchor tag to add the **target** attribute, like so:

```
<a href="http://www.alcatrazcruises.com/" target="_blank"><img src="images/
logo-alcatraz.jpg" class="img-left" alt="Alcatraz Cruises"></a>
```

4A Coding Links: Images & Page Jumps

7. Save the file and reload your page in a browser to test out the link once more. This time the link will open in a new tab. (If a user has set preferences for links to open in windows rather than tabs, a new window will open.)

8. Return to **sanfran.html** in your code editor. Let's use the same method for linking up the other two images in this section.

9. Find the image for **Fisherman's Wharf**, and wrap an anchor tag around it as shown below in bold:

```
<p><a href="http://www.fishermanswharf.org/" target="_blank"><img src="images/
logo-fishermans-wharf.jpg" class="img-right" alt="Fisherman's Wharf"></a>
```

10. Find the **Blazing Saddles** image, and wrap an anchor tag around it as shown below:

```
<p><a href="http://www.blazingsaddles.com/" target="_blank"><img src="images/
logo-blazing-saddles.jpg" class="img-left" alt="Blazing Saddles"></a>
```

11. Save the file and reload your page in a browser to test out the two new links. Each should open in its own new tab (or window).

Links Within a Page

In order to make navigating the content of a page easier, **IDs** can be coded into sections of the document and then links to those IDs can be provided from a "Table of Contents" of sorts. A visitor can simply click a link to jump down the page and view a section.

The content of the sanfran page has been set up to accommodate these types of "page jumps." Let's code it so it works.

1. In the **Things to Do** section, add an **ID** to the paragraph about **Alcatraz Island**, as shown below in bold:

```
<p id="alcatraz"><a href="http://www.alcatrazcruises.com/" target="_blank">
```

2. Let's do the same for the other two suggested activities. Add an ID to the paragraph about **Fisherman's Wharf**:

```
<p id="wharf"><a href="http://fishermanswharf.org/" target="_blank">
```

3. Add another ID to the **Blazing Saddles** paragraph:

```
<p id="biking"><a href="http://www.blazingsaddles.com/" target="_blank">
```

4. Just below that last paragraph, add one more ID to the **Local Travel Tips** heading:

```
<h2 id="tips">Local Travel Tips</h2>
```

5. Once an ID is added to a section of the page, you can link to it by making the ID the value of the href. Above the **Things to Do** section, next to **Jump to information about**, wrap the **Alcatraz** text with the following bold anchor tag and href to the ID of the section we want to jump to:

```
<p><em>Jump to information about:</em> <a href="#alcatraz">Alcatraz</a> |
Fisherman's Wharf
```

The **#** in the href tells the browser to find an element with that ID and scroll up or down to it.

6. While you're here, wrap another anchor around Fisherman's Wharf like so:

```
<a href="#wharf">Fisherman's Wharf</a>
```

7. Save the file and preview **sanfran.html** in a browser.

8. Click on your links to test them out. If the links do not work as expected, double-check the code. Make sure the **anchor's href** and the **ID** are typed the same and have no spaces or special characters.

9. Return to **sanfran.html** in your code editor and finish coding the remaining two links like so:

```
<a href="#biking">Bike Ride</a> | <a href="#tips">Local Travel Tips</a>
```

10. Save the file and reload your page in a browser to test the rest of the "page jumps."

11. The page jumps down to specific content nicely, but it would also be nice to be able to jump back up to the top of the document. Let's code that. Return to **sanfran.html** in your code editor.

12. Scroll down to the **Things to Do** section.

13. After the block of text about **Alcatraz**, you should see text that says, **Back to Top**. Wrap that text in an anchor tag with an href that points to **#** like so:

```
<a href="#">Back to Top</a></p>
```

You just created a link to an unnamed ID. When the browser encounters this, it jumps to the top of the document by default. Pretty neat trick.

14. Wrap the following three remaining **Back to Top** text phrases with the same exact `<a href="#">`Back to Top`</a>` code as you wrote in the previous step:

    • At the end of the **Fisherman's Wharf** content.

    • At the end of the **Blazing Saddles** content.

    • And all the way down at the end of the **Local Travel Tips** content (just above the **footer**).

    TIP: If you are using Sublime Text, you can select the first **Back to Top** you want to edit and then hit **Cmd–D** (Mac) or **Ctrl–D** (Windows) to add the next instance of Back to Top to the selection. (By doing this, you can make the same edits/additions to multiple sections of the code at once.) When all are selected, simply hit **Ctrl–Shift–W** (Mac) or **Alt–Shift–W** (Windows) to wrap your selection in the anchor tag.

15. Save the file and reload your page in a browser to test out all the **Back to Top** links!

16. Leave **sanfran.html** open. We'll continue with it in the next exercise.

17. If you finish early, check out the **Spambot Resistant Email Link** bonus exercise at the end of this book for more fun with links.

Styling Links

Exercise Preview

Featured Location: San Francisco, California

San Francisco is a beautiful city surrounded by the Pacific Ocean and San Francisco Bay. Its famous characteristics range from cable cars, to the Golden Gate Bridge, Alcatraz Island, Chinatown, Coit Tower, curvy Lombard Street, Victorian style homes and modern skyscrapers. The second most densely populated US city after New York, its weather is also unique. Most of the year San Francisco stays in the 60 degree range. During the spring and early summer, fog can cover portions of the city all day long.

Jump to information about: Alcatraz | Fisherman's Wharf | Bike Ride | Local Travel Tips

Things to Do

San Francisco is filled with culture, fine eating, nightlife and more. From beaches and parks, museums, bike riding, cable cars, to street performers, there is always something to do. The hard part is deciding how you'll spend your time! Here are a few recommendations:

Exercise Overview

The anchor tag has built-in style and functionality. When you code a link in HTML, the browser will render it with blue, underlined text. When a user clicks a link—while the link is pressed—the color of the text and the underline change to red. Once a link has been visited, the browser renders the link and underline in purple.

These styles offer solid, easily understood usability clues ("You are hovering over me. Please click on me!" or "Wait. You already saw that page."). That said, the browser's default colors and underline do not suit every design.

This exercise will show you how to create your own link styles and customize different link styles for different sections of the page.

1. If you completed the previous exercise, **sanfran.html** should still be open, and you can skip the following sidebar. If you closed **sanfran.html**, re-open it now from the **Revolution Travel** folder. We recommend you finish the previous exercises (3B–4A) before starting this one. If you haven't finished them, do the following sidebar.

> ### If You Did Not Do the Previous Exercises (3B–4A)
>
> 1. Close any files you may have open.
>
> 2. On the **Desktop**, go to **Class Files > yourname-Web Dev Class**.
>
> 3. Delete the **Revolution Travel** folder if it exists.
>
> 4. Duplicate the **Revolution Travel Ready for Styling Links** folder.
>
> 5. Rename the folder to **Revolution Travel**.

4B Styling Links

Creating a New Rule for the Anchor Tag

Let's begin by creating a new, default style for all links on the page. Since links are coded with the anchor tag <a>, we can do this quickly and easily with a tag selector.

1. In the styles at the top of **sanfran.html** add the following new rule just below the rule for **img**, like so:

```
img {
    max-width: 100%;
    border: 0;
}
a {
    color: #cf690b;
}
```

2. Save the file and preview it in a browser to see your change. It works! However, the underline doesn't work well in our design. Let's get rid of it.

3. Return to **sanfran.html** in your code editor and add the following property (in bold) to the rule for the anchor tag:

```
a {
    color: #cf690b;
    text-decoration: none;
}
```

4. Save the file and preview it in a browser to see your new link style.

5. Take a moment to mouse over and click on a couple of the links in the navigation, like **Tour Packages** or **Travel Tips**. Hit the **Back** button each time to return to the sanfran page.

6. Notice that the link style on **sanfran.html** stays exactly the same no matter how you interact with it. Let's take advantage of styling specific states of the anchor tag.

    TIP: Leave this page open in the browser so you can simply reload the page to see your new code as you work.

Pseudo-Classes

1. Return to **sanfran.html** in your code editor.

2. Edit the rule you just wrote for the anchor tag to add the **:link** pseudo-class
   as follows:

```
a:link {
    color: #cf690b;
    text-decoration: none;
}
```

   Notice the syntax of the selector. There is an additional **pseudo-class** being added to
   the tag, to target a specific behavior or functionality of that element. Pseudo-classes
   begin with a **colon (:)** and are written right next to the element you want to target,
   with no space between the element and the pseudo-class.

3. Save the file and preview it in a browser. Notice that links you have already visited
   are purple—the default color for visited links. That's because the level of specificity
   we just added with the pseudo-class tells the browser to only style links before they
   have been visited. Let's create our own style for visited links to override the purple
   default color.

4. Return to **sanfran.html** in your code editor.

5. Just below the **a:link** rule, add the following bold rule:

```
a:link {
    color: #cf690b;
    text-decoration: none;
}
a:visited {
    color: #666;
}
```

6. While we're here, let's add another rule to set the style of the link when a visitor
   clicks on the link. Just below the a:visited rule, add the following bold rule:

```
a:link {
    color: #cf690b;
    text-decoration: none;
}
a:visited {
    color: #666;
}
a:active {
    color: #ffcc00;
}
```

7. Save the file and preview it in a browser. Now the visited links are gray. Next, click
   and hold on any link to see that the active color is gold.

8. Hit the **Back** button to return to the sanfran page.

9. Let's create one last style that will indicate when a user's mouse is hovering over a link. Return to **sanfran.html** in your code editor.

10. Add the following bold rule below **a:visited** in the stack of link styles:

```
a:link {
   color: #cf690b;
   text-decoration: none;
}
a:visited {
   color: #666;
}
a:hover {
   color: #ffcc00;
   text-decoration: underline;
}
a:active {
   color: #ffcc00;
}
```

11. Save the file and preview it in a browser. Make sure to hover over the links to enjoy the new style.

Order Matters

The reason we had you write the stack of anchor rules in a specific order is because the order of your link styles, in particular, matters. Let's investigate.

1. Return to **sanfran.html** in your code editor.

2. Edit the stack of rules you just wrote for the anchor tag to move the **a:hover** rule above the a:visited rule, as follows:

```
a:link {
   color: #cf690b;
   text-decoration: none;
}
a:hover {
   color: #ffcc00;
   text-decoration: underline;
}
a:visited {
   color: #666;
}
a:active {
   color: #ffcc00;
}
```

3. Save the file and preview it in a browser. Make sure to hover over the links.

4. Take note of the fact that the hover rule is not working as expected when mousing over any visited links. The underline appears but the link stays gray instead of turning gold. Why is this?

The browser reads rules from the top down and all these rules have the same level of specificity, so the color for :visited is overriding the color for :hover. The order of link styles in the code matters! If they are out of order they may not work properly. If you want to properly style each different link state, the order should be:

- a:link

- a:visited

- a:hover

- a:active

Here's a trick to remember the order: LVHA, or LoVe/HAte.

5. Return to your code editor so we can put the rules for the links in the correct order again.

6. Edit the stack of rules for the anchor tag, as follows:

```
a:link {
    color: #cf690b;
    text-decoration: none;
}
a:visited {
    color: #666;
}
a:hover {
    color: #ffcc00;
    text-decoration: underline;
}
a:active {
    color: #ffcc00;
}
```

7. Let's also edit the rule for links before they have been visited. To make the code a little simpler, the :link pseudo-class does not really need to be stated directly; we can get the same results if we simply target all links and then add the rules for the specific :visited, :active, and :hover states. We can streamline the first rule in the stack as follows:

```
a {
   color: #cf690b;
   text-decoration: none;
}
a:visited {
   color: #666;
}
a:hover {
   color: #ffcc00;
   text-decoration: underline;
}
a:active {
   color: #ffcc00;
}
```

8. We can also get rid of the :active style. It's the same color as hover, so it's unnecessary at this point. Delete the rule for **a:active**. Your final stack of link styles should look like this when you are finished:

```
a {
   color: #cf690b;
   text-decoration: none;
}
a:visited {
   color: #666;
}
a:hover {
   color: #ffcc00;
   text-decoration: underline;
}
```

9. Save the file.

Adding a Class Selector for Quicklinks

Let's make one final stylistic tweak for the "page jump" link text.

Styling Links

1. Below the **.img-right** rule (at the bottom of the styles), add the following bold new rule. Be sure to keep it inside the closing `</style>` tag.

```
.quicklinks {
    font-family: Verdana, sans-serif;
    font-size: 12px;
}
</style>
```

2. Now we'll assign it to the paragraph that has the "page jump" links. Scroll down to the paragraph that says, **Jump to information about** and edit the following code:

```
<p class="quicklinks"><em>Jump to information about:</em>
```

3. Save the file, return to the browser, reload the page, and scroll down to see the new style.

4. You can keep **sanfran.html** open in the browser and the code editor. You'll continue with this file in the next exercise.

Exercise Preview

FEATURED LOCATION   TOUR PACKAGES   TRAVEL TIPS   ABOUT US   CONTACT

Featured Location: San Francisco, California

Exercise Overview

This exercise will show you how to style the list of links in the nav section so it looks more like a streamlined navigation bar and less like a clunky list of links. You'll also be introduced to descendant selectors: a way to target elements based on the semantic structure we created earlier.

1. If you completed the previous exercise, **sanfran.html** should still be open, and you can skip the following sidebar. If you closed **sanfran.html**, re-open it now. We recommend you finish the previous exercises (3B–4B) before starting this one. If you haven't finished them, do the following sidebar.

> **If You Did Not Do the Previous Exercises (3B–4B)**
>
> 1. Close any files you may have open.
>
> 2. On the **Desktop**, go to **Class Files > yourname-Web Dev Class**.
>
> 3. Delete the **Revolution Travel** folder if it exists.
>
> 4. Duplicate the **Revolution Travel Ready for Nav Styles** folder.
>
> 5. Rename the folder to **Revolution Travel**.

4C Styling the Navigation

Overriding Default List Styles

First things first: because we created a semantically correct list of links, the links have unsightly bullets next to them. Let's get rid of the bullets.

1. In **sanfran.html**, add the following new rule below the rule for **img**:

```
img {
    max-width: 100%;
    border: 0;
}
ul {
    list-style-type: none;
}
```

2. Save the file and preview **sanfran.html** in Chrome. (We will be using Chrome's DevTools window in this exercise. If you decide to use another browser, the steps will be similar.)

3. The navigation looks better already, but let's investigate further. **Ctrl–click** (Mac) or **Right–click** (Windows) in the nav and choose **Inspect**.

4. In the DevTools window, mouse over the **<ul>** tag and, as you do so, take a look at the way it is highlighted in the browser window above. You should see an orange-colored highlight above and below the list and a green highlight to the left of the list. The orange color indicates the margins of the element, while green indicates padding. Let's get rid of all this extra space.

NOTE: We recommend leaving **sanfran.html** open in Chrome as you work, so you can simply reload the page to see the changes you make in the code.

5. Return to **sanfran.html** in your code editor.

6. Edit the rule for **ul** to add the following property declarations:

```
ul {
    list-style-type: none;
    margin: 0;
    padding: 0;
}
```

7. Save the file, return to Chrome, and reload the page. Getting there! Next, we'd rather have a horizontal navigation than a vertical navigation for this site. List items display as stacked elements, so we'll have to modify their native display property.

8. Return to **sanfran.html** in your code editor.

9. Add the following new rule below the rule for **ul**:

```
ul {
    list-style-type: none;
    margin: 0;
    padding: 0;
}
li {
    display: inline;
}
```

10. Save the file, return to the browser, and reload the page. Easy! Next, we'll need some space between the list items. Let's add margin.

11. Return to **sanfran.html** in your code editor.

12. Add the following new property to the rule for **li**:

```
li {
    display: inline;
    margin-right: 20px;
}
```

13. Save the file, return to Chrome, and reload the page. Looking good.

Using Descendant Selectors

The rules we just wrote—for ul and li—are working out just fine for this particular page. But if there were another unordered list on the page, it would also be affected by these rules. Let's make our rules more specific to the navigation on the page.

1. Return to **sanfran.html** in your code editor.

2. Scroll down to the **nav** (just after the start of the **body** tag):

```
<nav>
   <ul>
      <li><a href="sanfran.html">Featured Location</a></li>
      <li><a href="packages.html">Tour Packages</a></li>
      <li><a href="tips.html">Travel Tips</a></li>
      <li><a href="about.html">About Us</a></li>
      <li><a href="contact.html">Contact</a></li>
   </ul>
</nav>
```

Notice that the list items sit inside the `<ul>` tag and the `<ul>` tag sits inside the `<nav>` element. We can use the **nav** as part of the selector to make sure our new rules will only affect the unordered list and list items in this particular section of the page.

3. Scroll back up to your styles. Edit the rules for **ul** and **li**, as follows:

```
nav ul {
   list-style-type: none;
   margin: 0;
   padding: 0;
}
nav li {
   display: inline;
   margin-right: 20px;
}
```

The selectors you just wrote are officially known as **descendant selectors**. The ul sits inside the nav, so the nav is a parent (or ancestor), and the ul is its child (or descendant). The logic holds true for the li as well. The li is the grandchild of the nav —a more distant descendant—but a descendant nonetheless.

4. Take a moment to check for typos. Note that there is a single **space** between the **nav** and descendant elements.

Styling the Navigation

4C

5. Let's organize the styles so these rules are grouped with the rule for **nav**. Cut both rules and paste them below the rule for **nav** (farther down in the styles). Your rules should look like the following example when you're finished:

```
nav {
    margin-bottom: 30px;
}
nav ul {
    list-style-type: none;
    margin: 0;
    padding: 0;
}
nav li {
    display: inline;
    margin-right: 20px;
}
main {
    width: 90%;
    max-width: 800px;
    display: block;
    margin-bottom: 30px;
}
```

6. Save the file.

Using Descendant Selectors to Style the Navigation

The link styles we created in an earlier exercise look fine for the links that sit in the main content of the document, but it would be nice to create a distinct style for the links in the navigation. Let's use descendant selectors again to get the job done.

1. Just below the rule for the **nav li** add the following new rule:

```
nav li {
    display: inline;
    margin-right: 20px;
}
nav a {
    font-size: 13px;
    color: #666;
    text-transform: uppercase;
}
```

2. Save the file and reload your page in the browser. Take a moment to scroll down and notice that these styles only affect the navigation anchors. The other links keep their original style. Nice!

WEB DEVELOPMENT LEVEL 1 • COPYRIGHT NOBLE DESKTOP

125

3. Mouse over the links in the nav to see the :hover styles we created earlier. Let's create a new :hover style that will be unique to the nav. Once again, descendant selectors will come in handy.

4. Return to **sanfran.html** in your code editor.

5. Add the following new rule below the rule for **nav a**:

```
nav a {
    font-size: 13px;
    color: #666;
    text-transform: uppercase;
}
nav a:hover {
    color: #13aad7;
    text-decoration: none;
}
```

6. Save the file and reload your page in the browser.

7. Make sure to hover over the links in the nav and compare to the :hover style in the links for for the rest of the page. Well done.

Improving the Usability of the Navigation Links

While still in the browser, scroll back up to the navigation and mouse over the links to test their usability. The clickable area is simply defined by the text-based content in the anchor. Let's make the clickable area larger.

1. Return to **sanfran.html** in your code editor.

2. Edit the **nav a** style to add a new declaration for padding, as follows:

```
nav a {
    font-size: 13px;
    color: #666;
    text-transform: uppercase;
    padding: 10px;
}
```

3. Save the file and reload your page in Chrome.

4. Mouse over the links in the navigation. The clickable area seems much more generous, but there's a CSS rendering issue we should address. Let's use the DevTools window to investigate.

5. **Ctrl–click** (Mac) or **Right–click** (Windows) on a link in the nav and choose **Inspect**.

6. In the DevTools window, click the **<a>** tag and take a look at the styles on the right. Click the checkbox next to padding to disable and enable this property a few times:

The top padding is not quite working as expected. You can see the links get farther apart horizontally but the links do not move 10 pixels down from the top as expected.

This is because anchor elements are displayed inline. Inline elements are designed to be unobtrusive in the layout and do not respond to height or vertical modifications in padding or margin. Let's modify the display property of the anchor element in the nav section.

7. Return to **sanfran.html** in your code editor.

8. Edit the **nav a** style to add a new declaration for display, as follows:

```
nav a {
    font-size: 13px;
    color: #666;
    text-transform: uppercase;
    padding: 10px;
    display: inline-block;
}
```

Using **inline-block** is a way to combine the best of both worlds: have block-level control over the padding but have the links display inline, horizontally across the top of the page.

9. Save the file and reload your page in Chrome. Feel free to inspect the links in the DevTools window to get a better sense of the padding.

Now that we've added padding around the links properly, there appears to be more space than we really need between the list items, the header, the nav, and the main content. Let's modify the rules for these elements to restore some balance to the spacing.

10. Return to **sanfran.html** in your code editor.

4C Styling the Navigation

11. Find the rule for **nav li** and **remove** the **margin-right** property declaration. When you're finished, your rule should read as follows:

```
nav li {
    display: inline;
}
```

12. A bit above that, edit the **margin-bottom** value for the **nav** rule as follows:

```
nav {
    margin-bottom: 10px;
}
```

13. Finally, edit the **margin-bottom** value for the **header** rule as follows:

```
header {
    margin-bottom: 10px;
    border-bottom: 1px solid #4a5f04;
    padding-bottom: 20px;
}
```

14. Save the file and reload the browser to see the improved spacing of the content.

15. You can keep **sanfran.html** open in the browser and the code editor. You'll continue with this file in the next exercise.

Exercise Preview

Exercise Overview

CSS styles can be embedded into individual webpages or shared across multiple pages. When working on a complete site, it makes sense to share the styles in order to have consistent styles across multiple pages. Sharing CSS not only makes changes easier to make later (because one change updates all linked pages) but it also reuses the code, making the website load faster.

1. If you completed the previous exercise, **sanfran.html** should still be open, and you can skip the following sidebar. If you closed **sanfran.html**, re-open it now. We recommend you finish the previous exercises (3B–4C) before starting this one. If you haven't finished them, do the following sidebar.

> **If You Did Not Do the Previous Exercises (3B–4C)**
>
> 1. Close any files you may have open.
>
> 2. On the **Desktop**, go to **Class Files > yourname-Web Dev Class**.
>
> 3. Delete the **Revolution Travel** folder if it exists.
>
> 4. Duplicate the **Revolution Travel Ready for Shared CSS** folder.
>
> 5. Rename the folder to **Revolution Travel**.

Creating & Linking to an External Style Sheet

First, let's move our embedded styles into an external style sheet so they can be shared across the entire site.

4D Shared CSS & Centering Content

1. In **sanfran.html** select **all** the rules inside the `<style></style>` tag. Start with the **body** rule and go all the way down to—and include—the closing curly brace of the **.quicklinks** rule.

2. Cut the rules (**Cmd–X** (Mac) or **Ctrl–X** (Windows)).

3. Open **main.css** in your code editor (it's in the **Revolution Travel** folder). This is a provided starter file that should not have any code yet.

4. Paste (**Cmd–V** (Mac) or **Ctrl–V** (Windows)) the rules. TIP: In Sublime Text, to paste the code so it matches your current indention level, you can press **Cmd–Shift–V** (Mac) or **Ctrl–Shift–V** (Windows) instead.

5. Save **main.css** and keep it open.

6. Return to **sanfran.html** in your code editor. Save the file.

7. Take a moment to preview this page (NOT main.css) in the browser to note what it looks like without its CSS.

   NOTE: Previewing a CSS file only shows the lines of code—with none of the HTML content it styles. So you don't accidentally preview main.css, we recommend leaving sanfran.html open in a browser so you can simply reload the page to test the code as you continue.

8. Return to **sanfran.html** in your code editor and delete the empty style tags:

   ```
   <style>

   </style>
   ```

9. Where the style tags used to be, type the following line of code:

   ```
   <link rel="stylesheet" href="main.css">
   ```

10. Note the required attributes of the **link** tag:

    • The **rel** attribute states the relationship of the linked document (it's a style sheet!)

    • The **href** provides the hyperlink reference to the style sheet file.

11. Save the file and reload your page in the browser to see how that one little line of code is pure magic. Your styles can now be shared across the other pages in the site as well.

    NOTE: Like images, the CSS file must be uploaded along with the HTML pages to your remote web server in order for visitors to see the styles.

Linking Styles to Other Pages

Now that we have styles in an external style file, we can share them across the entire site. Each page will have to be linked to the CSS file, but then we'll be able to edit styles for the entire site in one convenient file!

1. Return to your code editor.

2. Take a moment to select and copy (**Cmd–C** (Mac) or **Ctrl–C** (Windows)) the code you just wrote in **sanfran.html**:

   ```
   <link rel="stylesheet" href="main.css">
   ```

3. There should be six provided HTML files located in whichever Revolution Travel folder you are working in. (You may have already opened and edited the contact page in an earlier exercise.) There should be no styles—embedded or linked—in these files as of yet.

4. Open **about.html** in the code editor.

5. Paste the link code into the **head** tag of the document as shown:

   ```
   <head>
       <meta charset="UTF-8">
       <title>Revolution Travel - About Revolution Travel</title>
       <link rel="stylesheet" href="main.css">
   </head>
   ```

6. Save the file and then close the file.

7. With the code still copied on your clipboard, repeat steps 4–6 with the following files. Be certain to paste the link code after the title and above the closing head tag, as shown in the example above.

   - contact.html

   - index.html

   - tips.html

8. Make sure you saved all the files and closed them.

9. Open **packages.html** and paste the link code into the **head** tag of the document:

```
<head>
   <meta charset="UTF-8">
   <title>Revolution Travel - Featured Travel Packages</title>
   <link rel="stylesheet" href="main.css">
   <style>
      .featured-package {
         width: 33.333%;
         float: left;
         text align: center;
      }
      .clear-float {
         clear:both;
      }
   </style>
</head>
```

Note that this file has some embedded styles as well that apply to elements that only appear on this page. Make sure to paste the linked style sheet above the embedded styles as a best practice.

Linked Styles vs. Embedded Styles

Embedded styles can happily coexist with linked styles from an external style sheet. It's not an either/or proposition.

Although linked style sheets allow you to easily maintain a cohesive appearance for elements across a site, there may be elements on a single page that are not repeated elsewhere—as in this particular example—so the need to share these styles is not present.

Embedded styles may also be used to override rules from linked styles on a page-by-page basis. If you would like to embed styles to override rules in a shared style sheet, you must place the embedded styles below the link to the shared style sheet.

---

10. Save the file and then close it.

11. Go ahead and preview any HTML page (i.e. NOT main.css) in the browser and test out your links. Enjoy the look and feel of the shared style sheet. Keep the browser open to any of these pages so you can simply reload the browser to test the code as you continue.

Shared CSS & Centering Content

Centering the Logo & Nav Content

Let's center the logo in the header per the design specification.

1. Open **main.css** in your code editor (if it's not already open).

2. Find the rule for **header** and add the following property declaration (in bold):

```
header {
    margin-bottom: 10px;
    border-bottom: 1px solid #4a5f04;
    padding-bottom: 20px;
    text-align: center;
}
```

> ### The Text-Align Property
>
> Although images are—obviously—not text, they are **inline** elements. Inline
> elements like text, anchor tags, and images will be placed horizontally in a
> line, rather than stacking like blocks (as paragraphs, headings, and divs do).
> All inline elements can be aligned horizontally using CSS's text-align property.

3. Save the file.

4. Reload any of the site's pages in the browser to see the centered logo. Pretty easy!

   One change to one CSS file is shared across all the HTML pages that link up to it.
   Let's center the content in the navigation the same way.

5. Return to **main.css**.

6. In the **nav** rule, add the **text-align** property (in bold):

```
nav {
    margin-bottom: 10px;
    text-align: center;
}
```

7. Save the file, return to the browser, and reload the page to see how the logo and
   your nav center up in the browser window.

Centering the Page Content

It would be great if we could change the rest of the content to a centered format.
Thanks to our shared CSS, one modification will affect the entire site.

1. Return to **main.css** in your code editor.

2. In the **main** rule, add the following new properties (in bold):

```
main {
    width: 90%;
    max-width: 800px;
    display: block;
    margin-bottom: 30px;
    margin-left: auto;
    margin-right: auto;
}
```

3. Save the file and reload any of the site's pages in a browser. Notice that all the main content is centered across the board. Amazing.

   Remember: To center an element, simply set a width for the element and then specify the margins on the left and the right to be **auto** for automatic. The effect horizontally centers the element with respect to the edges of the body of the document.

4. Return to **main.css** in your code editor and edit the **footer** rule to center it as well:

```
footer {
    width: 90%;
    max-width: 800px;
    margin-left: auto;
    margin-right: auto;
}
```

5. Save the file and reload any of the site's pages to see the improved layout.

Fine-Tuning Margins & Padding

The border below the header section will look a whole lot more elegant if we remove the pesky white margin on the left and the right.

The margin is there because the body element is rendered in all major browsers with about 8px of margin by default. This puts space between the edge of the browser window and the content of the page. To close up that space, let's redefine the body tag with a new rule for margin.

1. Return to **main.css** in your code editor.

2. Go to the very top and edit the rule for **body** as follows:

```
body {
    font-family: sans-serif;
    font-size: 16px;
    line-height: 24px;
    margin: 0;
}
```

3. Save the file and reload any of the site's pages in a browser to see the changes to the margin around the content of the page.

   The border now touches the edges of the browser window, which is an improvement, but the logo could use a little breathing room on top. Let's edit the header to add some padding on top to complement the padding we have on the bottom.

4. Return to your code editor and add padding-top to the **header** rule as follows:

```
header {
    margin-bottom: 10px;
    border-bottom: 1px solid #4a5f04;
    padding-top: 20px;
    padding-bottom: 20px;
    text-align: center;
}
```

5. Save the file and reload any of the site's pages in a browser to enjoy the improved header.

Fine-Tuning Heading Styles with Grouped Selectors

1. While still in the browser, take a look at the headings. The text is bold because browsers style headings this way by default. It's a little heavy-handed, though. Let's modify it.

2. Return to **main.css** in your code editor.

3. Edit the heading styles as follows:

```
h1 {
    font-size: 28px;
    color: #6a8e6b;
    line-height: 30px;
    font-weight: normal;
}
h2 {
    font-size: 18px;
    color: #6a8e6b;
    font-weight: normal;
}
```

4. Save the file and reload any of the site's pages in a browser to see the improved headings.

5. Return to your code editor.

6. Take a second look at the rules for the headings. There are a couple of redundancies here that can be improved. When selectors share the same properties, they can be grouped into a comma-separated list.

7. Add the following new rule above the rule for **h1**:

```
h1, h2 {
    color: #6a8e6b;
    font-weight: normal;
}
h1 {
```

8. Edit the rules for **h1** and **h2** to delete the color and font-weight properties, as you no longer need to repeat these. Your final rules for headings should be as follows:

```
h1, h2 {
    color: #6a8e6b;
    font-weight: normal;
}
h1 {
    font-size: 28px;
    line-height: 30px;
}
h2 {
    font-size: 18px;
}
```

9. Save the file.

Styling the Footer Content

The copyright content shouldn't necessarily be as prominent as the other text-based content on the page. Let's write a style to mute the copyright text color and also offset this content a bit.

1. In the **footer** rule (near the bottom), add the following new properties:

```
footer {
    width: 90%;
    max-width: 800px;
    margin-left: auto;
    margin-right: auto;
    font-family: Arial, Helvetica, sans-serif;
    color: #999;
    font-size: 12px;
    text-transform: uppercase;
}
```

2. Save the file and reload any of the site's pages to see the amended copyright text in the footer. Let's place a subtle border between the copyright content in the footer and the page content.

3. Return to **main.css** in your code editor and continue to edit the rule for footer to add the following new border property:

```
footer {
```
(CODE OMITTED TO SAVE SPACE)
```
    text-transform: uppercase;
    border-top: 1px solid #ddd;
}
```

4. Save the file and reload any of the site's pages to see the footer's border. Let's push the border away from the footer content a bit more.

5. Return to **main.css** in your code editor and edit the footer to add the following padding property:

```
footer {
```
(CODE OMITTED TO SAVE SPACE)
```
    border-top: 1px solid #ddd;
    padding-top: 20px;
}
```

6. Save the file and reload any of the site's pages to see the enhanced separation of the footer content. Let's create the same style between page topics.

7. Edit the **h2** rule (near the top) to add the following properties (in bold):

```
h2 {
    font-size: 18px;
    border-top: 1px solid #ddd;
    padding-top: 20px;
}
```

8. Save the file and reload any of the site's pages to see the finished design.

9. You can keep these files open in the browser and the code editor. You'll continue with this site in the next exercise.

How to Create a Brand New CSS File

In Sublime Text & Most Code Editors:

1. Go to **File > New File**.

2. Save the file as **main.css** (or another name of your choosing), and you're all set to start coding styles.

In Dreamweaver:

1. Go to **File > New**.

2. Select **New Document** (used to be **Blank Page**) and Document Type: **CSS**.

3. Hit **Create**. You're all set to start coding styles.

Setting the Viewport Meta Tag

Exercise Preview

Featured Location: San Francisco, California

Exercise Overview

The viewport meta tag controls how a webpage is displayed on a mobile device. Without the viewport set, mobile devices will render the page at a typical desktop screen width, scaled to fit the screen. Setting a viewport gives control over the page's width and scaling on different devices.

1. If you completed the previous exercise, you can skip the following sidebar. If you closed **sanfran.html**, re-open it now. We recommend you finish the previous exercises (3B–4D) before starting this one. If you haven't finished them, do the following sidebar.

> ### If You Did Not Do the Previous Exercises (3B–4D)
>
> 1. Close any files you may have open.
>
> 2. On the **Desktop**, go to **Class Files > yourname-Web Dev Class**.
>
> 3. Delete the **Revolution Travel** folder if it exists.
>
> 4. Duplicate the **Revolution Travel Ready for Viewport** folder.
>
> 5. Rename the folder to **Revolution Travel**.

The Viewport Meta Tag

While the webpage responds beautifully in the browser, in order to test how it will actually look on a mobile device, we need to use an emulator. Thankfully, Chrome provides a mobile emulator in the Developer Tools.

1. Preview **sanfran.html** in Chrome.

2. To open the DevTools, **Ctrl–click** (Mac) or **Right–click** (Windows) on the page and choose **Inspect**.

3. At the top left of the DevTools window, click the **Toggle device toolbar** button ⬚:

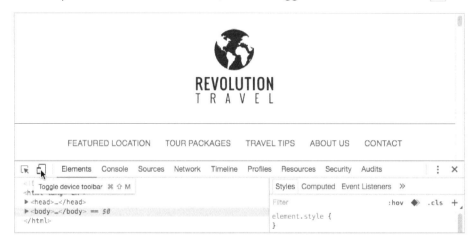

4. In the emulator (shown below), choose a device to emulate. We recommend choosing a popular device such as the **iPhone 6** (or 5) or **Galaxy S5**.

5. Reload the page to make sure it's displayed properly.

6. The content does not look optimized for a mobile device. It looks like a wide desktop page that has been scaled down to fit on a small mobile screen.

Mobile browsers employ a default width and scaling behavior. Small devices assume sites were designed for desktops. They render the page at a large desktop screen width and scale it down to fit the smaller screen. We must use a viewport meta tag to tell it to render the page at the pixel width of the device. This will prevent it from zooming out so far.

7. Return to **sanfran.html** in your code editor.

8. In the **<head>** tag, add the following bold code:

```
<head>
   <meta charset="UTF-8">
   <title>Revolution Travel - Travel Info for San Francisco, CA</title>
   <meta name="viewport" content="">
   <link rel="stylesheet" href="main.css">
</head>
```

NOTE: Like other meta tags, this tag always goes in the head of the document. This meta tag is generally referred to as the viewport meta tag or simply viewport tag.

9. The content attribute of the tag can take a few comma-separated key-value pairs for different settings. Add the following bold code:

```
<meta name="viewport" content="width=device-width">
```

NOTE: **width=device-width** tells the browser to set the width of the viewport to the available width of the device.

10. Save the file.

11. Return to Chrome and reload the page in the emulator mode. The code we added won't make any visual change to what you see in a desktop browser, only in a mobile browser which employs a default scaling behavior. As shown below, on the left is how the page used to look, and on the right we see that the width of the page is now set to the device's width and looks correct!

Setting Initial Scale

1. What happens when we rotate the device to landscape? In the Chrome DevTools emulator, click the **Rotate** button ◇ in the top toolbar.

All looks fine in Chrome, where the portrait layout is recalculated to show more content in the wider, landscape preview.

2. If you were to view this rotated page in some other browsers (such as iOS 8 Safari and Windows Phone) the layout would be scaled up to fill the wider screen.

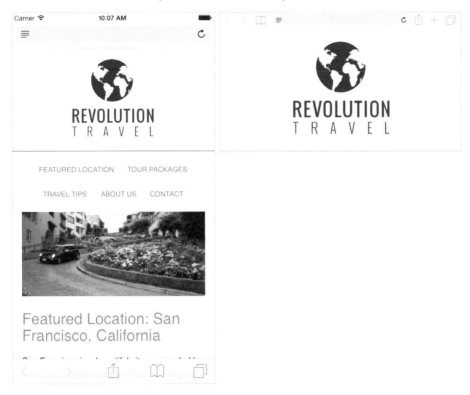

In these browsers, you actually see less of the page when you rotate your device. Most users would probably expect to see more of the page. This is easy to fix. We can control the initial scale of a page.

NOTE: iOS 9 changed this behavior so it acts like Chrome.

3. Back in **sanfran.html**, add the following bold code and don't miss the comma!

```
<meta name="viewport" content="width=device-width, initial-scale=1">
```

NOTE: Initial-scale represents a scaling (or zoom) ratio. Setting **initial-scale=1** tells the browser to set the scale/zoom of the page to 100%, which is the same as not scaling/zooming the page at all. A value of 1.5 would set the page to a scale/zoom of 150%.

4. Save the file.

NOTE: This meta tag needs to be present on every page of the website. If you finish early, feel free to copy the meta tag and paste it into the <head> section of the other pages in the Revolution Travel site.

5. If you were to preview **sanfran.html** in iOS 8 Safari or Windows Phone once again, you would notice you now have a wider page. The page items remain the same size and are not zoomed, so you can see more content. We think most users would expect this behavior:

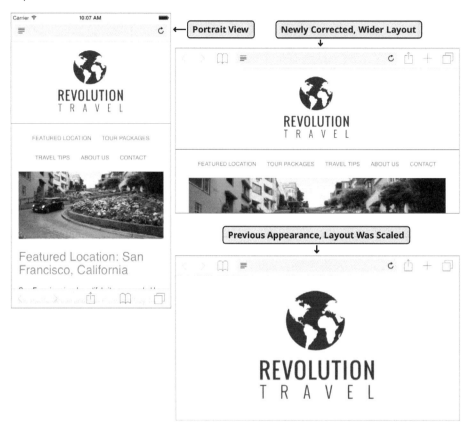

6. You may close all opened files in the code editor and the browser if you like now. You have completed the Revolution Travel site—congratulations!

Disabling Zoom

Mobile browser users can zoom in on a page. Adding **maximum-scale=1** to the viewport meta tag limits how far a user can zoom in. When the maximum-scale and the initial-scale are both set to 1, the user will be unable to zoom. It also does not work in all browsers though (such as Safari on iOS, which ignores this code so users can still zoom).

While it's possible to disable page zooming, we do not recommend it. It doesn't work everywhere, and if type is not large enough, it can be hard to read and users will not be able to enlarge it! Not everyone has 20/20 vision.

Exercise Preview

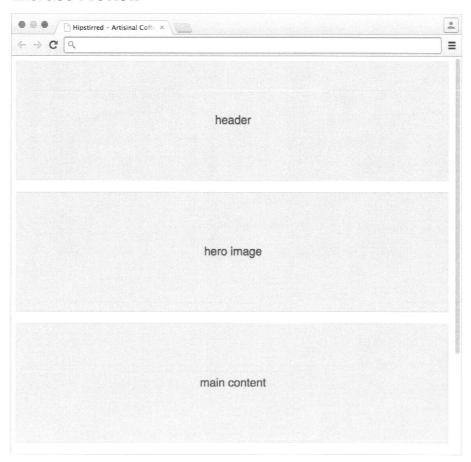

Exercise Overview

This is the first in a series of exercises where we'll build a mini-site to announce a product launch. This is a service that is planning a soft-launch via sign up codes. There will be a home page, a sign up page with a basic form, and a thank-you page to confirm the form submission.

It's often helpful to see the informational hierarchy of the site and plan the layout before you incorporate the actual content, so we'll start with a wireframe for the home page. You will simply set up the content structure in this exercise and label the semantic sections accordingly. We'll use some basic CSS to help visually delineate the sections of the page but the final content, styles, and images will be fleshed out in the following exercises.

5B HTML & CSS Wireframe

Getting Started

1. We'll be using a new folder of provided files for this exercise. This website folder contains images and some code snippets of tagged HTML content for you to use. Close any files you may have open in your code editor to avoid confusion.

2. For this exercise we'll be working with the **Hipstirred Wireframe** folder located in **Desktop > Class Files > yourname-Web Dev Class**.

   TIP: It's beneficial to see the entire website folder as you work. Many code editors allow you to do so. If you're in Sublime Text, go to **File > Open** (Mac) or **File > Open Folder** (Windows), navigate to **Class Files > yourname-Web Dev Class > Hipstirred Wireframe** and hit **Open** (Mac) or **Select Folder** (Windows).

3. In your code editor, open **index.html** from the **Hipstirred Wireframe** folder.

4. Title the document by editing the code as follows:

   ```
   <title>Hipstirred - Artisanal Coffee Curators</title>
   ```

Coding Up the Sections

The home page will feature a header, a prominent hero section where the headings will overlay an image background, a main content section that describes the product, and a footer that will contain the copyright and social media links.

1. Add the following sectioning tags (highlighted in bold) inside the body tag:

   ```
   <body>
       <header></header>
       <div></div>
       <main role="main"></main>
       <footer></footer>
   </body>
   </html>
   ```

   NOTE: We're using a **div** element for the hero image section of the page. There is no available semantic tag to describe this kind of content, so this is the most appropriate method.

2. If you were to preview in a browser, you wouldn't see a thing. By default, section elements have no border, no background, and are only as tall as the content inside. Let's add some text to describe the sections. Add the following content:

   ```
   <header>header</header>
   <div>hero image</div>
   <main role="main">main content</main>
   <footer>footer</footer>
   ```

3. Save the file and preview **index.html** in Chrome (we'll be using Chrome's DevTools). If you use another browser, the steps may differ slightly. There's not much to see by way of structure. Let's add some CSS to flesh out these sections.

NOTE: We recommend leaving **index.html** open in Chrome as you work, so you can reload the page to see the changes you make in the code.

Creating a Placeholder Style

1. Return to your code editor.

2. Open **main.css** from the **Hipstirred Wireframe** folder. The provided file is completely empty. Let's start by declaring some basic font defaults for the page.

3. Create the following new rule in **main.css**:

```css
body {
    font-family: sans-serif;
    color: #555;
}
```

4. Next, we can create a placeholder style for all the sections to share. We'll use this until we're ready to style each section more specifically. Add the following new rule just below the rule for **body**:

```css
.placeholder {
    background-color: #ddd;
    border: 1px solid #ccc;
    display: block;
}
```

NOTE: This placeholder rule will be used for all elements in the layout. Because we are using the <main> element, we need to give Internet Explorer (IE) a hand here and let it know to display **main** as a block element, so we can style it accordingly. (The **main** element is properly supported in Microsoft Edge, the browser that replaces IE starting with Windows 10).

5. Save **main.css**.

Linking to an External Style Sheet

1. Return to **index.html**.

2. Add a link to **main.css**, as follows:

```
<head>
    <meta charset="UTF-8">
    <title>Hipstirred - Artisanal Coffee Curators</title>
    <meta name="viewport" content="width=device-width, initial-scale=1">
    <link rel="stylesheet" href="main.css">
</head>
```

3. As shown below, add a placeholder class to each of the section elements. TIP: Some code editors (such as Sublime Text) let you create multiple cursors by holding **Cmd** (Mac) or **Ctrl** (Windows) as you click. You could put a cursor on each tag and then type **class="placeholder"** in only once!

```
<header class="placeholder">header</header>
<div class="placeholder">hero image</div>
<main class="placeholder" role="main">main content</main>
<footer class="placeholder">footer</footer>
```

4. Save **index.html**.

5. Return to Chrome and reload the page. Getting closer, but let's make the text more prominent. We could also use some space between the sections.

6. Return to your code editor and switch to **main.css**.

7. Add the following new properties to the rule for **.placeholder**:

```
.placeholder {
    background-color: #ddd;
    border: 1px solid #ccc;
    display: block;
    font-size: 20px;
    text-align: center;
    margin-bottom: 20px;
}
```

8. Save **main.css**.

9. Return to Chrome and reload **index.html**. Better. It would be nice to add some height to the sections, though, to flesh them out a bit. We can achieve this goal with a few different CSS properties. Let's take a moment to investigate.

10. Return to **main.css** in your code editor.

11. Add the following new property to the rule for **.placeholder**:

```
.placeholder {
   background-color: #ddd;
   border: 1px solid #ccc;
   display: block;
   font-size: 20px;
   text-align: center;
   margin-bottom: 20px;
   height: 200px;
}
```

12. Save **main.css**.

13. Return to Chrome and reload **index.html**. Not bad, but it would be nice if the text were vertically centered in the box. Let's try padding instead. Padding, as you recall, also visually opens up an element's box by making it appear wider and/or taller.

14. Return to **main.css** in your code editor.

15. Edit the **height** property to change it to **padding** instead:

```
.placeholder {
   background-color: #ddd;
   border: 1px solid #ccc;
   display: block;
   font-size: 20px;
   text-align: center;
   margin-bottom: 20px;
   padding: 200px;
}
```

16. Save **main.css**.

17. Return to Chrome and reload **index.html**. Woah. That's huge. Our text is now centered vertically because we have the same amount of padding on top and on bottom, but 200px of padding makes these boxes much bigger than we need for the wireframe. Let's take a closer look at this in Chrome's DevTools.

18. To inspect these placeholder sections in DevTools, **Ctrl–click** (Mac) or **Right–click** (Windows) on the text that says **header** and choose **Inspect**.

19. If you're still in device mode, click the **Toggle device toolbar** button ⬚ at the top left of the DevTools.

20. In the Elements tab, scroll over the **\<header\>** tag to see how it's highlighted in the browser. The green color shows the padding and the orange color shows the margin. Note, too, that Chrome shows the height of the element: 425px:

How does the browser calculate the height of the element where padding is concerned? 200 pixels of padding on top and bottom should add up to 400 pixels, but this is taller. That's because padding is added to the content height (borders also add to an element's visual size). Let's use the DevTools to see this more closely.

21. On the right side of the DevTools window, switch from the Styles tab to the **Computed** tab. You'll see a diagram of the box model for the header element:

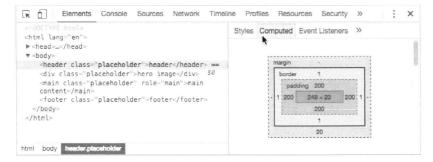

Notice how the content sits in the center (248 x 23 in the screenshot above). Padding surrounds the content, and the border sits at the edge of the padding. Feel free to hover over each part of the box model to see it selected in the browser.

22. Return to **main.css** in your code editor. Let's try one more method of opening up these sections of the wireframe.

23. Edit the **padding** property to change it to **line-height** instead:

```
.placeholder {
    background-color: #ddd;
    border: 1px solid #ccc;
    display: block;
    font-size: 20px;
    text-align: center;
    margin-bottom: 20px;
    line-height: 200px;
}
```

24. Save **main.css**.

25. Return to Chrome and reload **index.html**. Nice. A cool feature of line-height is that, because the height is evenly distributed above and below the text, the text is vertically centered within that height. (It works differently in print design, where it's called leading and goes below the baseline of text, to replicate the way lead strips used to be placed below lines of metal type in the days of hand-typesetting.)

26. If you closed DevTools, **Ctrl–click** (Mac) or **Right–click** (Windows) on the text that says **header** and choose **Inspect**. Scroll over the **<header>** tag to see how it's highlighted in the browser. Notice that it's only 202 pixels tall now, the line-height value plus the 1-pixel border on the top and the bottom. Pretty neat.

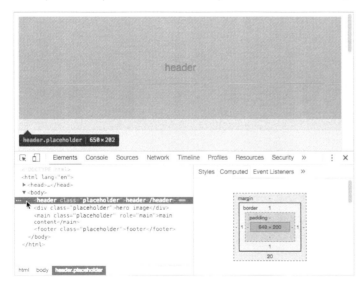

27. Nothing has been styled yet, so the content just stacks in a logical order and is fluid within the confines of the browser window. You'll add content and style in the exercises that follow.

CSS Background Images

Exercise Preview

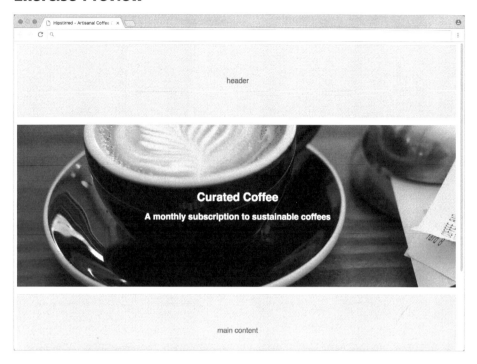

Exercise Overview

We're going to continue to build a mini-site to announce a product launch. We'll start with the wireframe for the home page from the previous exercise. In addition to a standard header, footer, and main content, the home page will feature a prominent hero section where the headings will overlay an image background. In this exercise, we'll focus on the hero section of the page and, as we style it, take a deep dive into the CSS background-image property.

1. We'll be using a new folder of provided files for this exercise. Close any files you may have open in your code editor to avoid confusion.

2. For this exercise we'll be working with the **Hipstirred Hero** folder located in **Desktop > Class Files > yourname-Web Dev Class**. You may want to open that folder in your code editor if it allows you to (like Sublime Text does).

3. Open **index.html** from the **Hipstirred Hero** folder.

4. Preview **index.html** in Chrome. (We will be using Chrome's DevTools window in this exercise. If you decide to use another browser, the steps will be similar.)

   NOTE: We recommend leaving **index.html** open in the browser as you work, so you can simply reload the page to see the changes you make in the code.

5C CSS Background Images

Adding the Hero Content

Traditionally, the hero section of a webpage is the most prominent content a user will see when they visit the page. A hero image often consists of a large image and text, and its purpose is to give an overview of the site's most important theme or content. Heading levels 1 and 2 are best used to describe a short overview of this nature, so let's code up some headings in this section.

1. Return to your code editor.

2. Find the **<div>** on line 11. Delete the words **hero image** and open up the <div></div> tag as follows:

```
<body>
    <header class="placeholder">header</header>
    <div class="placeholder">

    </div>
    <main class="placeholder" role="main">main content</main>
    <footer class="placeholder">footer</footer>
</body>
```

3. Add the following content to the **<div>**:

```
<div class="placeholder">
    <h1>Curated Coffee</h1>
    <h2>A monthly subscription to sustainable coffees</h2>
</div>
```

4. Save **index.html**.

5. Return to Chrome and reload **index.html**. Okay. Those headings are pretty far apart. We still have the **.placeholder** style associated with this section and that style used line-height to open up the space. Let's get rid of **.placeholder** and create a new style specifically for this section.

Creating a Hero Style

1. Return to **index.html** in your code editor.

2. Modify the class attribute of the <div> as follows:

```
<div class="hero">
    <h1>Curated Coffee</h1>
    <h2>A monthly subscription to sustainable coffees</h2>
</div>
```

3. Save **index.html**.

4. Open **main.css** from the **Hipstirred Hero** folder.

5. We want to center the text in the hero, maintain a margin of 20 pixels on the bottom, add some space inside the div, and keep the gray background so we can see the size of the section we're working with. Create the following new rule below **.placeholder**:

```
.hero {
    text-align: center;
    margin-bottom: 20px;
    padding-top: 30px;
    padding-bottom: 30px;
    background-color: #ddd;
}
```

NOTE: In an earlier exercise, we saw that we could increase the height of a div with either CSS height, line-height, or padding. Because we want to keep the text nicely centered vertically, but don't want to affect the spacing between the lines of text, padding will do the trick nicely here.

6. Save **main.css**.

7. Return to Chrome and reload the page. Better. Now let's pretty things up with a background graphic.

Adding a CSS Background-Image

Before we add our hero photo, let's see how CSS background images can be used to create a repeating pattern. We'll start with a graphic (shown below) that is a single 60px by 60px square image.

1. Return to **main.css** in your code editor.

2. Add the following new property to the **.hero** rule:

```
.hero {
    ( CODE OMITTED TO SAVE SPACE )

    background-color: #ddd;
    background-image: url(images/pattern.png);
}
```

3. Let's also change the text to white, so it's more legible on the darker background:

```
.hero {
   color: #fff;
   text-align: center;
```

4. Save **main.css**.

5. Return to Chrome and reload the page. Notice the original square graphic appears at its native size, but then repeats (in rows and columns) to fill the entire space of the containing div.

6. Resize the browser window to see the pattern is cropped by the containing div. The pattern size remains constant, but how many rows and columns of repeats you see is determined by the size of the containing div.

7. Let's switch to our hero image. Return to **main.css** in your code editor.

8. In the **.hero** rule, change the background image to the hero photo:

```
.hero {

   ( CODE OMITTED TO SAVE SPACE )

   background-image: url(images/hero-flat-white.jpg);
}
```

9. Save **main.css**.

10. Return to Chrome, reload the page, and note the following:

   • Unlike the small pattern, this hero photo is very large. Only the top left of the photo is visible. We'll have to make the containing div taller to see more of the photo. If you could go behind the scenes, you'd see that the top left of the large image is behind the two headings, as illustrated below:

   • It's hard to see, but the photo does appear at its native size and then repeats. You'll only be able to see the repeat (on the right side) on larger monitors.

CSS Background Images

Modifying Background-Position

1. We can modify the CSS to move the position of the image behind the hero div. Let's use DevTools to preview our code changes as we make them. While still in Chrome, **Ctrl–click** (Mac) or **Right–click** (Windows) on the hero section and choose **Inspect**.

2. In the Elements panel, select the **hero** div (you'll see it highlighted in the browser):

```
    ⌖  ⎙       Elements   Console   Sources   Network   Timeline   Profiles
    <!DOCTYPE html>
    <html lang="en">
    ▶ <head>…</head>
    ▼ <body>
        <header class="placeholder">header</header>
  ···▼ <div class="hero"> == $0
          <h1>Curated Coffee</h1>
          <h2>A monthly subscription to sustainable coffees</h2>
        </div>
        <main class="placeholder" role="main">main content</main>
        <footer class="placeholder">footer</footer>
      </body>
    </html>
    html   body   div.hero   h1
```

3. You should now see the **.hero** rule in the **Styles** tab on the right side of the DevTools window. Click at the bottom of the stack of property declarations for the **.hero** rule. The cursor should be blinking, indicating that you're ready to start typing to add a new property declaration:

```
  Styles  Computed  Event Listeners  DOM Breakpoints  Properties
  Filter                               :hov  ◆  .cls  +
  element.style {
  }
  .hero {                                         main.css:14
  ☑ color: ☐#fff;
  ☑ text-align: center;
  ☑ margin-bottom: 20px;
  ☑ padding-top: 30px;
  ☑ padding-bottom: 30px;
  ☑ background-color: ☐#ddd;
  ☑ background-image: url(images/hero-flat-white.jpg);
     |;
  }
```

4. Type **background-position: right bottom** into the DevTools window:

```
  .hero {                                         main.css:14
  ☑ color: ☐#fff;
  ☑ text-align: center;
  ☑ margin-bottom: 20px;
  ☑ padding-top: 30px;
  ☑ padding-bottom: 30px;
  ☑ background-color: ☐#ddd;
  ☑ background-image: url(images/hero-flat-white.jpg);
     background-position: right bottom;
  }
```

5. You can see the image move behind the headings in the hero div as you modify the CSS in the DevTools window. Excellent!

   NOTE: The background-position property takes two values: the X position (horizontal offset) and the Y position (vertical offset) separated by a space. The default value is **left top**. Values can be keywords **top**, **bottom**, **left**, **right**, and **center**, but you can also use absolute pixel values or percentages (which we'll experiment with a bit later).

6. Click on the **right bottom** value of the **background-position** property and change it to **center center** (the image should center within the hero section both horizontally and vertically).

Opening Up the Hero Section

1. Let's create a larger "window" through which we can see the photo. Return to **main.css** in your code editor.

2. In the **.hero** rule, change the padding to **160px**:

   ```
   .hero {
       color: #fff;
       text-align: center;
       margin-bottom: 20px;
       padding-top: 160px;
       padding-bottom: 160px;
       background-color: #ddd;
       background-image: url(images/hero-flat-white.jpg);
   }
   ```

3. While we're here, let's also officially set the background-position to **left center** as shown below:

   ```
   background-image: url(images/hero-flat-white.jpg);
   background-position: left center;
   }
   ```

4. Save **main.css**.

5. Return to Chrome and reload the page. Better. The size of the hero section and the position of the image looks good but the white text would look a bit nicer on the dark part of the cup, rather than in the lighter foam (and the photo is still repeating on larger monitors). Let's use the DevTools inspector to fine-tune the position.

Discovering Background-Repeat

1. **Ctrl–click** (Mac) or **Right–click** (Windows) on the hero section and choose **Inspect**.

CSS Background Images

2. In the Elements panel, select the **hero** div.

3. In the **Styles** tab, find the **.hero** rule.

4. Click on the **left center** value of the **background-position** property and change it to **200px 100px**. Interesting!

   Now that we've offset the X and Y position, you can certainly see that the background-image is repeating (like a pattern). We do not want the photo to repeat, so let's modify this in our CSS file. We can come back to fix the position a bit later.

5. Return to **main.css** in your code editor.

6. Add the following new property declaration to the **.hero** rule:

   ```
   background-image: url(images/hero-flat-white.jpg);
   background-position: left center;
   background-repeat: no-repeat;
   }
   ```

   NOTE: You can also set **background-repeat** to **repeat-x** (creates a row of repeating images horizontally) or **repeat-y** (creates a column of repeating images vertically).

7. Save **main.css**.

8. Return to Chrome and reload **index.html**. Now the image will only show once even if we were to modify the background-position. This is better, but we want a flexible image that will scale with the hero section.

Setting the Background-Size

1. Expand and contract the browser window to see that the image does not scale. If possible, extend the window wider than the native 1280 pixels of the image we're using. You'll see that we run out of image here and we're left with just the gray background of the hero section. Let's use background-size to remedy this.

2. Return to **main.css** in your code editor.

3. Add the following new property declaration to **.hero**:

   ```
   background-image: url(images/hero-flat-white.jpg);
   background-position: left center;
   background-repeat: no-repeat;
   background-size: 100% auto;
   }
   ```

   The background-size property accepts a width (first value) and height (second value) separated by a space. We can use fixed pixel sizes for the image or percentages that correspond to the background positioning area. Here, we're setting the background image to be 100% of the width of the hero section and using **auto** for the height to maintain the aspect ratio.

4. Save **main.css**.

5. Return to Chrome and reload the page. Experiment with the width of the browser window to see how the background scales. It looks great on a wide window, but when the browser window is narrow, the height adjusts to maintain the aspect ratio and the gray background shows us that the image does not fill the space as well as we'd like.

6. Return to **main.css** in your code editor.

7. Let's try to fill the height of the hero. Edit the background size property value as follows:

```
background-size: 100% 100%;
}
```

8. Save **main.css**.

9. Return to Chrome and reload the page. Experiment with the width of the browser window again. Yikes. The image now squishes to fit the hero area. Not the look we want. Let's try out a couple of keywords that can be of great help.

10. Return to **main.css** in your code editor.

11. Edit the background size property value as follows:

```
background-size: contain;
}
```

12. Save **main.css**.

13. Return to Chrome and reload the page. Again, not what we're after. But in some cases, **contain** can be a handy value to use. The keyword **contain** scales the image as large as possible and maintains the image's aspect ratio. What we're looking to do here is keep as much of the image as possible in the sweet spot of the hero area, maintain the aspect ratio, and possibly just crop what's left over if necessary. The keyword for this is **cover**. Let's try it.

14. Return to **main.css** in your code editor.

15. Edit the background size property value as follows:

```
background-size: cover;
}
```

16. Save **main.css**.

17. Return to Chrome and reload the page. Make sure to experiment with the width of the browser window. Wonderful! This looks pretty nice. We're finally ready to move the image so the headings are over the cup rather than in the foam.

Perfecting the Background-Position

1. Make the browser window fairly wide.

2. **Ctrl–click** (Mac) or **Right–click** (Windows) on the hero section and choose **Inspect**.

3. In the Elements panel, select the **hero** div.

4. Find the **.hero** rule in the **Styles** tab.

5. Click on the **left center** value of the **background-position** property and change it to **center 0%**

6. Now highlight just the **0%** value.

7. Hold **Shift** and press the **Up Arrow** key on your keyboard to increase the value **10** percent at a time. Find a value that positions the image nicely behind the header. At a wider screen size, around 70–80% seems to work well. On a smaller screen, the text will be atop the foam. It will still work, though it will be more ideal on the desktop.

   NOTE: Percentage values are relative to the background positioning area. 0% 0% is the left top. 100% 100% is the right bottom. 50% 50% is center center. We set the Y offset to 75% to move the image up slightly higher, so we see more of the bottom part of the image.

8. Return to **main.css** in your code editor to lock this change into the final code.

9. Edit the background-position property value for the **.hero** rule as follows:

   ```
   background-position: center 75%;
   background-repeat: no-repeat;
   background-size: cover;
   }
   ```

10. Save **main.css**.

11. Return to the browser, reload the page, and enjoy your hero image!

Fun with Fonts

Exercise Preview

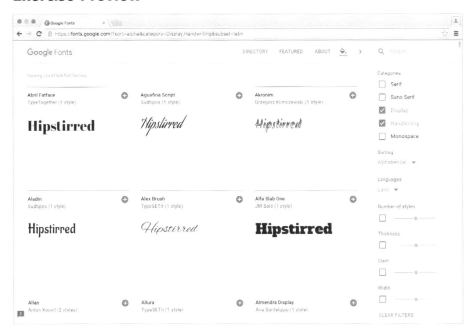

Exercise Overview

In this exercise, we'll continue with the mini site. We'll add the logo and the text-based content to the project, and review CSS font properties. We'll also give the page a more polished, professional look by embedding custom fonts rather than sticking to the safe, bland list of fonts that ship with most operating systems. We'll use **Google Fonts**, the industry leader in free web fonts. Google hosts hundreds of fonts and provides the code to make it all work. Let's get started.

1. We'll be using a new folder of provided files for this exercise. Close any files you may have open in your code editor to avoid confusion.

2. For this exercise we'll be working with the **Hipstirred Font Fun** folder located in **Desktop > Class Files > yourname-Web Dev Class**. You may want to open that folder in your code editor if it allows you to (like Sublime Text does).

3. Open **index.html** from the **Hipstirred Font Fun** folder.

Experimenting with Google Fonts

This brand would do well with a simple typographic logo. Let's use Google Fonts to experiment with some ideas. First, we need to get rid of the placeholder class and add real content to the header.

1. On the `<header>` tag, delete `class="placeholder"`

2. Inside the **\<header\>** tag, delete the word **header**, and add the paragraph shown below in bold:

```
<header>
   <p class="logo">Hipstirred</p>
</header>
```

NOTE: We'll use the **logo** class temporarily to style the text in the paragraph.

3. Save **index.html** and preview the page in a browser to see what we have so far. Plain and simple. Let's give this brand more of an identity.

NOTE: We recommend leaving **index.html** open in the browser as you work, so you can simply reload the page to see the changes you make in the code.

4. In a new browser tab, go to fonts.google.com

5. In the sidebar on the right, we can filter by **Categories** to find a suitable font. We're looking for something impactful and quirky. **Uncheck** all the categories except **Display** and **Handwriting**.

6. In the sidebar below the Categories, change the **Sorting** menu to **Alphabetical**.

7. Google Fonts are used in countries that have different scripts, such as India. To hide those fonts, change the **Languages** menu to **Latin**.

8. We want to preview our specific **Hipstirred** text, so select any one of the example texts and type **Hipstirred** over it.

9. To change all the previews to that text, at the bottom right of your font preview, click **APPLY TO ALL FONTS** (as shown below):

10. Take a moment to scroll through a few of the available fonts.

11. We have three fonts specific fonts we want to try. The fonts are in alphabetical order, so scroll to find **Cookie**.

12. To the right of **Cookie**, click the ⊕ button:

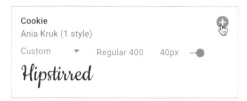

A bar should appear at the bottom of the page that says you have
1 Family Selected.

13. In the search field at the upper right of the page, search for **Pacifico**.

14. To the right of **Pacifico**, click the ⊕ button.

15. Search for **Sacramento** and click its ⊕ button.

16. At the bottom, click anywhere on the bar that says **3 Families Selected** to display
more options about your selection.

17. Click on the **CUSTOMIZE** tab.

Here you choose which styles you need for each family. For Cookie, Pacifico, and
Sacramento, **regular** is the only style option for each, but other fonts may have bold,
italic, etc.

NOTE: When deciding on which styles to include, keep in mind that each style will
increase the file size and slightly slow down the loading of the page (as indicated by
the **Load Time** estimate). Only load styles you will actually be using.

18. Switch back to the **EMBED** tab.

19. Under **Embed Font**, copy the link to the external style sheet that is hosted
by Google:

```
<link href="https://fonts.googleapis.com/css?family=Cookie|Pacifico|
Sacramento" rel="stylesheet">
```

20. Return to **index.html** in your code editor.

21. Paste the link below the viewport meta tag and above the link to main.css, as shown
in bold below:

```
<meta name="viewport" content="width=device-width, initial-scale=1">
<link href="https://fonts.googleapis.com/css?family=Cookie|Pacifico|
Sacramento" rel="stylesheet">
<link rel="stylesheet" href="main.css">
```

NOTE: Some browsers will not display text until its font has been downloaded.
Putting the link to Google Fonts before links to other CSS files will start the font
download as soon as possible.

22. Save the file.

5D Fun with Fonts

Adding Fonts to the Page

1. We're ready to start experimenting with these fonts. Open **main.css**.

2. At the bottom, create the following new rule:

   ```
   .logo {

   }
   ```

3. Return to Google Fonts in the browser.

4. Under **Specify in CSS**, copy the code for the **Sacramento** font:

   ```
   font-family: 'Sacramento', cursive;
   ```

5. Close the Google Fonts browser tab.

6. You should still have **index.html** open in the browser. Leave it open so you can reload the page to see the changes you make in the code.

7. Return to **main.css** in your code editor.

8. Paste the code you copied into the rule for **.logo**, and notice it has the name of the custom font as the first choice as well as a fallback:

   ```
   .logo {
       font-family: 'Sacramento', cursive;
   }
   ```

9. We're just experimenting with fonts for now, but if we were going to use a style like this in our final code, we don't recommend using cursive as a fallback. There aren't any consistent, common cursive fonts used on Mac and Windows, so it could fall back to Comic Sans or Brush Script or something even worse! Frankly, we'd rather fall back to Helvetica or Arial if our custom font doesn't load. Edit the font stack for good measure:

   ```
   font-family: 'Sacramento', sans-serif;
   ```

10. Save **main.css**.

11. Return to the browser and reload **index.html**. Adorable, but a little small and it could be darker.

12. Return to **main.css** in your code editor.

13. Edit the rule for **.logo** to increase the font-size and change the color as follows:

    ```
    .logo {
        font-family: 'Sacramento', sans-serif;
        font-size: 35px;
        color: #000;
    }
    ```

14. Save **main.css**.

15. Return to the browser and reload **index.html**. Better! But maybe not as impactful as it could be.

16. Return to **main.css** in your code editor.

17. Edit the rule for **.logo** to try **Pacifico** instead:

```
.logo {
    font-family: 'Pacifico', sans-serif;
    font-size: 35px;
    color: #000;
}
```

18. Save **main.css**.

19. Return to the browser and reload **index.html**. Bolder! But maybe too large and loopy?

20. Return to **main.css** in your code editor.

21. Let's give **Cookie** a try:

```
font-family: 'Cookie', sans-serif;
```

22. Save **main.css**.

23. Return to the browser and reload **index.html**. This seems right on.

Using an Image for the Logo

While it may seem tempting to leave things as is for the Hipstirred logo, it's important to understand that Google Fonts are not as bulletproof as we would like them to be for something as crucial as a logo. Corporate, campus, or even government regulation firewalls that are particularly aggressive can block Google Fonts. For instance, in China, users will have to enjoy Hipstirred in Helvetica or Arial because Google Fonts are definitely blocked there.

That doesn't mean the exercise was moot! Web fonts can be fun and useful for rapid prototyping, as we just did with the logo.

1. Return to your code editor and switch to **index.html**. We've created an image for you to use in place of the plain text.

2. **Delete** the paragraph in the header and replace it with an image:

```
<header>
   <img src="images/hipstirred-logo.png" height="36" width="105"
alt="Hipstirred">
</header>
```

NOTE: We're coding a width and height for this logo because it's always going to be a fixed size in the layout. If the size was going to be flexible, we'd omit the height and width as we saw earlier.

3. Save the file and return to the browser to reload the page and see the logo. The space is tighter because the margins from the paragraph are no longer there. We'll adjust the spacing later.

How to Use Google Fonts on the Desktop

If you need to use Google web fonts while designing in desktop apps like Photoshop, Sketch, or Adobe XD, you can download Google fonts using **SkyFonts**. SkyFonts is a free app from Monotype that allows you to quickly install Google fonts (and more) onto your Mac or PC. Another benefit is that whenever fonts are updated on Google Fonts, SkyFonts automatically updates the fonts installed on your system as well!

Find out more at **fonts.com/web-fonts/google**

Styling the Main Content

We can also successfully embed fonts for the main content, where fallback fonts in the font stack will be perfectly acceptable should Google Fonts fail.

1. Return to **index.html** in your code editor.

2. To save you some time, we've tagged up the main content for the page and saved it into a file. Open **main-content.html** from the **snippets** folder (in the **Hipstirred Font Fun** folder).

3. Select all the code (**Cmd–A** (Mac) or **Ctrl–A** (Windows)).

4. Copy it (**Cmd–C** (Mac) or **Ctrl–C** (Windows)).

5. Close the file.

6. You should be back in **index.html**.

7. Delete the words **main content** between the **<main>** opening and closing tags. Then to make our code more legible, hit **Return** (Mac) or **Enter** (Windows) to place the closing </main> tag on its own line like so:

```
<main class="placeholder" role="main">

</main>
```

8. Now paste (**Cmd–V** (Mac) or **Ctrl–V** (Windows)) the code you just copied into the **main** section. TIP: In Sublime Text, to paste the code so it matches your current indention level, press **Cmd–Shift–V** (Mac) or **Ctrl–Shift–V** (Windows) instead.

9. Find the last paragraph in the main content: **<p>© hipstirred LLC</p>**.

10. Cut it (**Cmd–X** (Mac) or **Ctrl–X** (Windows)).

11. Paste the copyright paragraph into the **footer**, replacing the text that was there:

```
<footer class="placeholder">
   <p>© hipstirred LLC</p>
</footer>
```

12. Save the file.

13. Return to the browser to reload the page and preview the content. Yowza. That placeholder line-height is not going to work here.

14. Return to **index.html** in your code editor.

15. Delete the two remaining instances of **class="placeholder"**

16. Save the file.

17. Return to the browser to reload the page and preview the content. The text is fine but uninspiring. Let's find a better font.

Getting a Different Google Font

1. In a new browser tab, go to fonts.google.com

2. In the search field on the top right, search for **Open Sans**.

3. To the right of **Open Sans**, click the ⊕ button.

4. At the bottom, click on the **1 Family Selected** bar.

5. Instead of just sticking with the **regular** style, let's add a **light** style. Click on the **CUSTOMIZE** tab.

6. Check the box next to **light 300**.

7. Go back to the **EMBED** tab.

5D Fun with Fonts

8. Under **Embed Font**, copy the link to Google's external style sheet:

   ```
   <link href="https://fonts.googleapis.com/css?family=Open+Sans:300,400"
   rel="stylesheet">
   ```

9. Close the Google Fonts browser tab.

10. You should still have **index.html** open in the browser. Leave it open so you can reload the page to see the changes you make in the code.

11. Return to **index.html** in your code editor.

12. Delete the current Google Fonts link and paste the new one in the same place (as shown below in bold):

    ```
    <meta name="viewport" content="width=device-width, initial-scale=1">
    <link href="https://fonts.googleapis.com/css?family=Open+Sans:300,400"
    rel="stylesheet">
    <link rel="stylesheet" href="main.css">
    ```

13. Save the file.

14. Switch to **main.css** and edit the rule for **body** as follows:

    ```
    body {
        font-family: 'Open Sans', sans-serif;
        color: #555;
    }
    ```

15. While we're here, let's get rid of the styles we no longer need. **Delete** both the rule for **.placeholder** and the rule for **.logo**. Your style sheet should now just have two rules: one for **body** and one for **.hero**.

16. Save the file.

17. Return to the browser to reload **index.html** and preview the content. Classy! We just need to fine-tune some of the text styles.

Improving the Heading Styles

1. Return to **main.css** in your code editor.

2. The main heading in the hero section could be more prominent. Add the following new rule below the **body** rule:

   ```
   body {
       font-family: 'Open Sans', sans-serif;
       color: #555;
   }
   h1 {
       font-size: 64px;
   }
   ```

3. Save the file and reload **index.html** in the browser to preview the change. A little too prominent. Instead of changing the size, though, let's use the **Light 300** font style we embedded. The number **300** can be used as a value for font-weight to access this lighter style.

4. Return to **main.css** in your code editor.

5. Add the following new property declaration to the **h1** rule:

```
h1 {
    font-size: 64px;
    font-weight: 300;
}
```

6. Save the file and reload **index.html** in the browser to preview the change. Sleek. The second-level heading should be a bit smaller and lighter as well, but also provide balance for the large, open main heading. A light-weight, smaller font-size with uppercase letters will do the trick nicely.

7. Return to **main.css** in your code editor.

8. Add the following new rule below the **h1** rule:

```
h1 {
    font-size: 64px;
    font-weight: 300;
}
h2 {
    font-size: 16px;
    font-weight: 300;
    text-transform: uppercase;
}
```

9. Save the file and reload **index.html** in the browser to preview the change. This has promise, but the headings are too far apart. Let's make the main heading's default margin smaller.

Improving Line-Height & Margin

1. Return to **main.css** in your code editor.

2. Add the following new property declaration to the **h1** rule:

```
h1 {
    font-size: 64px;
    font-weight: 300;
    margin-bottom: 0;
}
```

3. Save the file and reload **index.html** in the browser to preview the change. Make your browser window fairly wide. Nice! But take a moment to make the browser window narrow enough so **Curated** and **Coffee** each go on a separate line. Not so nice:

4. The line-height needs to be tightened up. Return to **main.css** in your code editor.

5. Add the following new property declaration to the **h1** rule:

```
h1 {
    font-size: 64px;
    font-weight: 300;
    line-height: 64px;
    margin-bottom: 0;
}
```

6. Save the file and reload **index.html** in the browser to preview the change. Make sure to expand and contract the browser window to test the new line-height. Looks good. Now let's style the level-3 headings to create more obvious topic breaks.

7. Return to **main.css** in your code editor.

8. Add the following new rule below the **h2** rule:

```
h2 {
    font-size: 16px;
    font-weight: 300;
    text-transform: uppercase;
}
h3 {
    font-size: 22px;
    border-bottom: 1px solid #ddd;
    padding-bottom: 10px;
}
```

9. Save the file and reload **index.html** in the browser to preview the refined headings. The paragraphs could also use spacial refinement. They're not very legible.

10. Return to **main.css** in your code editor.

11. Let's open up space between paragraphs. Add the following new rule for **p** below the **h3** rule:

```
p {
    margin-bottom: 30px;
}
```

12. Save the file.

13. Return to the browser to reload **index.html** and preview the change. Hmmm. That's only marginally better (pun intended). What we really need to do is improve the space between the lines of text. Let's modify the line-height.

14. Return to **main.css** in your code editor.

15. Add the following new declaration to the **paragraph** rule:

```
p {
    margin-bottom: 30px;
    line-height: 40px;
}
```

16. Save the file.

17. Return to the browser to reload **index.html**. This seems more spacious and legible overall, particularly at a tablet-sized page width or smaller. But if you open up the browser width, these long lines of text are hard to read.

    We need to set a maximum width for the layout to improve the usability of this page. We'll tackle this problem in the next exercise!

    Testing Google Fonts

    When embedding fonts from Google Fonts, or any other font hosting service, we recommend that you test the site in as many browsers as possible as well as on another computer to be sure your fonts are loading correctly. If you have the fonts installed in your system, you may mistakenly think you have embedded fonts correctly when you have not because your browser will naturally be able to show your system fonts. Additionally, it's a good idea to test thoroughly because fonts may render in your browser a bit differently than they would in a user's browser where the fonts are not installed.

Hipstirred Layout: Fine-Tuning with the Box Model

6A

Exercise Preview

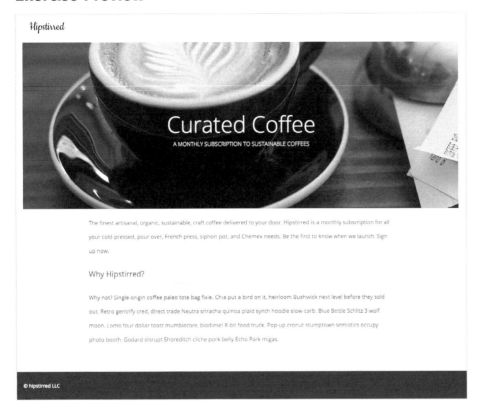

Exercise Overview

In this exercise, we will refine the spacing and dimensions of the layout for the mini site and revisit the handy CSS max-width property. Along the way, we'll investigate wrapping content in container divs and firm up our understanding of how an ID selector differs from a class selector.

1. We'll be using a new folder of provided files for this exercise. Close any files you may have open in your code editor to avoid confusion.

2. For this exercise we'll be working with the **Hipstirred Box Model** folder located in **Desktop > Class Files > yourname-Web Dev Class**. You may want to open that folder in your code editor if it allows you to (like Sublime Text does).

3. Open **index.html** from the **Hipstirred Box Model** folder.

4. Preview **index.html** in Chrome to see what we have so far. (We will be using Chrome's DevTools window in this exercise. If you decide to use another browser, the steps will be similar.)

   We have a lovely, fluid layout for the page, but there have been no widths declared for any of the sections, and the text content gets far too wide. The header could use a bit of padding, as the logo is a little hemmed in. We'd also like the hero section and the footer to extend to the edge of the browser window. Let's add some style to the footer to see how well this section extends edge to edge.

   NOTE: We recommend leaving **index.html** open in Chrome as you work, so you can simply reload the page to see the changes you make in the code.

Styling the Footer

1. Return to your code editor and open **main.css**.

2. Add a new rule for **footer** just below the **p** rule:

```
footer {
    background-color: #3e2d20;
}
```

3. Save **main.css**.

4. Return to the browser and reload **index.html**. Scroll down to preview the footer. The text is a bit large for a copyright. It's also too dark for this background. Let's make the text smaller, give it a light color, and open up this element's box with some padding. The footer could stand to be a bit meatier.

5. Return to **main.css** in your code editor.

6. Edit the rule for **footer** as follows:

```
footer {
    color: #fff;
    font-size: 14px;
    padding: 20px;
    background-color: #3e2d20;
}
```

7. Save **main.css**.

8. Return to Chrome and reload **index.html**. The footer is nice and tall now, but taller than expected. In fact, the copyright paragraph doesn't look centered vertically. What's going on? Let's inspect.

9. **Ctrl–click** (Mac) or **Right–click** (Windows) on the footer and choose **Inspect**.

10. In the Elements panel, select the **<p>** tag. You'll see it highlighted in the browser and you should also see the **p** rule in the **Styles** tab on the right side of the DevTools window:

The margin values we want for most of the paragraphs are too large here in the footer. Luckily descendant selectors allow us to target an element when it's inside of another element. We want to style the **p** tags only inside the **footer**.

11. Return to **main.css** in your code editor.

12. Add a new rule below the rule for **footer** as follows:

```
footer {
    color: #fff;
    font-size: 14px;
    padding: 20px;
    background-color: #3e2d20;
}
footer p {
    margin: 0;
}
```

13. Save **main.css**.

14. Return to the browser and reload **index.html**. It works perfectly. Now let's get rid of the margins around the edges of the page.

Removing Margin from the Body

The hero section and footer will look a whole lot more elegant if we remove the white margin around them.

The margin is there because the body element is rendered in all major browsers with about 8px of margin by default. This puts space between the edge of the browser window and the content of the page. To close up that space, let's edit the body rule.

1. Return to **main.css** in your code editor.

2. Edit the rule for **body** as follows:

```
body {
    font-family: 'Open Sans', sans-serif;
    color: #555;
    margin: 0;
}
```

3. Save **main.css**.

4. Return to the browser and reload **index.html**. Enjoy your edge-to-edge hero image and footer.

Giving the Logo Some Breathing Room

While the hero section and footer look great, the rest of the content shouldn't be right up against the edge of the browser window. We need to manage the space a bit more. Let's start with the header. The logo is way too tight against the top-left edge.

1. Return to **main.css** in your code editor.

2. Add the following new rule below the rule for **p**:

```
p {
    margin-bottom: 30px;
    line-height: 40px;
}
header {
    padding: 20px;
}
```

3. Save **main.css**.

4. Return to the browser and reload **index.html**. Looking good.

Reining in the Main Content

The main content is barely legible for two reasons: it's flush against the edge of the browser window, and it gets far too wide to read when the browser window is expanded. Let's see how we can tackle both these issues.

1. Return to **main.css** in your code editor.

2. Add the following new rule below the rule for header:

```
header {
    padding: 20px;
}
main {
    width: 70%;
    display: block;
}
```

NOTE: Remember that we need to set **main** to display as a block element so our styles will render appropriately in Internet Explorer (IE).

3. Save **main.css**.

4. Return to the browser and reload **index.html**. The text seems far more legible at this width but the main content should be centered in the page.

5. Return to **main.css** in your code editor.

6. Add the following new property to the rule for main:

```
main {
    width: 70%;
    display: block;
    margin-right: auto;
    margin-left: auto;
}
```

7. Save **main.css**.

8. Return to the browser and reload **index.html**. The page is shaping up nicely.

9. Expand your browser as wide as it will go. This is a great layout for a screen resolution of 1280 pixels or less. But if you were to open up the browser wider than this, you'd see that the image and text keep expanding out to the point where the layout is not very user-friendly. Go ahead and try it, if your resolution allows.

Setting Limits with an Outer-Wrapper & Max-Width

The easiest way to control the overall layout of the page is to wrap a `<div>` around all the content and then set limits to its width in the CSS.

1. Return to your code editor and switch to **index.html**.

2. Wrap a **div** tag around all the content of the document inside the **body** tag.

TIP: If Emmet is installed in your code editor, you can quickly wrap a selection by pressing **Ctrl–W** (Mac) or **Ctrl–Shift–G** (Windows). Then type in the wrapper (which in this case is **div**) and hit **Return** (Mac) or **Enter** (Windows).

3. When you're finished, check that you have an opening **\<div\>** (highlighted below in bold) just below the opening **body** tag.

```
<body>
   <div>
      <header>
         <img src="images/hipstirred-logo.png" height="36" width="105"
alt="Hipstirred">
```

4. Check that you have a closing **\</div\>** (highlighted below in bold) just above the closing **body** tag.

```
      <footer>
         <p>© hipstirred LLC</p>
      </footer>
   </div>
</body>
</html>
```

5. Give the \<div\> an ID of **wrapper**:

```
<body>
   <div id="wrapper">
      <header>
         <img src="images/hipstirred-logo.png" height="36" width="105"
alt="Hipstirred">
```

6. Save **index.html**.

7. Switch to **main.css** in your code editor.

8. Add the following new rule for **#wrapper** at the bottom of the file:

```
#wrapper {
   max-width: 1100px;
}
```

9. Save **main.css**.

10. Return to the browser and reload **index.html**. Experiment with making your browser narrow and wide. You'll see the content stop scaling up when you get to 1101 pixels or wider. It works! But the content isn't centered.

11. Return to **main.css** in your code editor.

12. Add the following new property to the rule for #wrapper:

```
#wrapper {
   max-width: 1100px;
   margin-right: auto;
   margin-left: auto;
}
```

13. Save **main.css**.

14. Return to the browser and reload **index.html**. Excellent. Make sure to scroll down to the footer, though. Awkward. Although we'd like the copyright content to have a max-width, the background color would look nicer stretching edge-to-edge.

Setting an Inner-Wrapper

1. Return to your code editor and switch to **index.html**.

2. What we need to do is end the current wrapper's `</div>` just after the `</main>` section and leave the footer out of the wrapper. Move the **</div>** as follows:

```
       </main>
   </div>
       <footer>
           <p>© hipstirred LLC</p>
       </footer>
   </body>
```

3. Save the file and return to the browser to reload the page and see your change. Scroll down to see that the footer is no longer constrained. We'd still like to have the copyright content align on the left with the Hipstirred logo, though. To accomplish this, we just need to place a wrapper around the content **inside** of the footer.

4. Return to **index.html** in your code editor.

5. As shown in bold, wrap a `<div>` tag around the **<p>** inside the `<footer>` and give it an ID of **wrapper**:

```
<footer>
    <div id="wrapper">
        <p>© hipstirred LLC</p>
    </div>
</footer>
```

6. Save the file and return to the browser to reload the page and see your change.

It worked but only because the browser is giving us a pass right now. We used the same ID twice, which goes against spec. We're seeing a "silent failure," which means that we have written invalid code, but the browser will try to guess what our intent was and handle it accordingly.

6A   Hipstirred Layout: Fine-Tuning with the Box Model

ID Selectors vs. Class Selectors

IDs signify uniqueness. They are meant to be used just once, per element, per page. Although the browser fails "silently" right now, this issue can come back to cause us problems down the road. Since the class selector was created specifically to style multiple elements the same way, let's use a class for wrapper instead of an ID.

1. Return to **index.html** in your code editor.

2. Scroll up to the first **wrapper** and edit the attribute as follows:

```
<body>
   <div class="wrapper">
      <header>
         <img src="images/hipstirred-logo.png" height="36" width="105" alt="Hipstirred">
```

3. Down in the footer, change **id** to **class** as well:

```
<footer>
   <div class="wrapper">
      <p>© hipstirred LLC</p>
   </div>
</footer>
```

4. Save the file and switch to **main.css**.

5. Change the id selector for **#wrapper** to make it a class selector, as follows:

```
.wrapper {
   max-width: 1100px;
   margin-right: auto;
   margin-left: auto;
}
```

6. Save the file and return to the browser to reload the page. If all goes well, you won't see any change but you can bask in the glow of your valid HTML and CSS.

Real-World Widths

We set the max-width value to 1100 pixels to make it easy to see max-width in action, even if you are working with a smaller resolution. For real-world design, though, we recommend setting a max-width to a more standard resolution, like 1280 pixels. This gives these users the edge-to-edge look we desire but also caps off the content when it gets too wide for users who have a higher resolution.

1. Return to **main.css** in your code editor. We'll set the max-width to be a more generous size.

2. Edit the value for the **max-width** property for **.wrapper** as follows:

```
.wrapper {
   max-width: 1280px;
   margin-right: auto;
   margin-left: auto;
}
```

3. Save **main.css**.

4. Return to the browser and reload **index.html**. If your screen is 1280px wide or less, the hero image should fill the page. If your screen is wider than 1280px, test out the new max-width value. Super!

Screen Resolution Statistics

The best way to find out who's looking at your site, what browser they're using, what their screen resolution is, where they live, and almost anything else you'd like to know, is to use Google Analytics, the industry standard for data. Google Analytics is free, though they have tiered pay plans for "enterprise-scale" data.

Find out more at **google.com/analytics**

If your site is not yet up and running, though, a good resource for web analytics is StatCounter. It's free and can give you a global picture of what's happening on the web.

Find out more at **gs.statcounter.com**

CSS Buttons & Floats

Exercise Preview

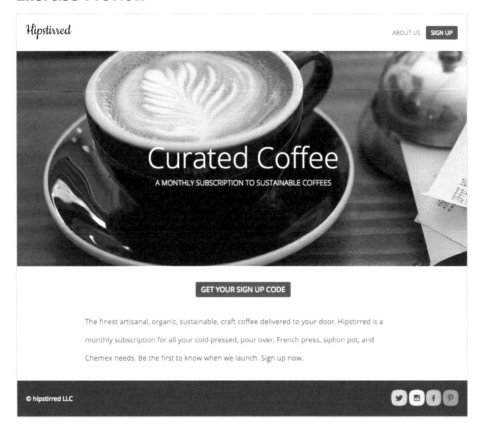

Exercise Overview

In this exercise, you will extend your knowledge of CSS navigation styles. You'll review semantically correct markup for navigation, learn about CSS border-radius for rounding corners, and learn how to create a handy, reusable button class. What's more, you'll learn how to make a more complex layout by using floats to pull elements to the far left or far right of the layout.

1. We'll be using a new folder of provided files for this exercise. Close any files you may have open in your code editor to avoid confusion.

2. For this exercise we'll be working with the **Hipstirred Buttons and Floats** folder located in **Desktop > Class Files > yourname-Web Dev Class**. You may want to open that folder in your code editor if it allows you to (like Sublime Text does).

3. Open **index.html** from the **Hipstirred Buttons and Floats** folder.

4. Preview **index.html** in Chrome. (We will be using Chrome's DevTools window in this exercise. If you decide to use another browser, the steps will be similar.)

   NOTE: We recommend leaving **index.html** open in the browser as you work, so you can simply reload the page to see the changes you make in the code.

6B CSS Buttons & Floats

Adding Navigation to the Header

1. Return to **index.html** in your code editor.

2. Add the following code inside the `<header>` below the `<img>` tag:

```
<header>
    <img src="images/hipstirred-logo.png" height="36" width="105"
alt="Hipstirred">
    <nav>

    </nav>
</header>
```

3. Add an unordered list with two list items inside the `<nav>`, as follows:

```
<nav>
    <ul>
        <li>about us</li>
        <li>sign up</li>
    </ul>
</nav>
```

4. Add links with placeholder hrefs around the text in each list item, as follows:

```
<nav>
    <ul>
        <li><a href="#">about us</a></li>
        <li><a href="#">sign up</a></li>
    </ul>
</nav>
```

5. Save the file and return to the browser to reload the page. While we understand the semantic value of providing a list of links, the style leaves a lot to be desired. Let's create a better look for the navigation.

6. Return to your code editor and open up **main.css**.

7. To remove the default bullets, margin, and padding from the unordered list, we should write a descendant selector. This way we know we'll specifically target unordered lists in the navigation and nowhere else on the site. Add the following new rule below the rule for header, as follows:

```
header {
    padding: 20px;
}
nav ul {
    list-style-type: none;
    margin: 0;
    padding: 0;
}
```

8. Save the file.

9. Return to the browser to reload **index.html**. Getting better. Let's override the default link styles here.

10. Return to **main.css** in your code editor.

11. We should write another descendant selector that specifically targets links in the navigation. This will ensure that link styles elsewhere won't be affected. Add the following new rule below the rule for nav ul, as follows:

```
nav ul {
    list-style-type: none;
    margin: 0;
    padding: 0;
}
nav a {
    color: #555;
    text-decoration: none;
}
```

12. Save the file.

13. Return to the browser to reload **index.html**. Getting better. Let's make the list items go horizontal rather than stack. The inline-block display property will be perfect.

14. Return to **main.css** in your code editor.

15. Add the following new rule below the rule for nav ul, as follows:

```
nav ul {
    list-style-type: none;
    margin: 0;
    padding: 0;
}
nav li {
    display: inline-block;
}
```

16. Save the file.

17. Return to the browser to reload **index.html**. Cool. What would look really nice, though, is if these links were tucked up to the right of the page above the hero image, rather than taking up space below the logo. CSS floats can be used for just this purpose.

Floats for Layout

1. Return to **main.css** in your code editor.

2. Add the following new rule above the rule for nav ul, as follows:

```
nav {
    float: right;
}
nav ul {
```

3. Save the file.

4. Return to the browser to reload **index.html**. That was easy. In fact, it was so easy, let's try it again for the footer.

Floating Social Media Links in the Footer

1. Return to your code editor.

2. To save you some time, we've provided you with the footer content. Open **footer-content.html** from the **snippets** folder in the **Hipstirred Buttons and Floats** folder.

3. Select all the content.

4. **Copy** it and close the file.

5. Switch to **index.html**.

6. Find the **footer** (near the bottom) and paste the content you just copied after the copyright paragraph, as follows:

```
<footer>
    <div class="wrapper">
        <p>© hipstirred LLC</p>
        <div class="social">
          <img src="images/twitter.png" height="36" width="36" alt="twitter">
          <img src="images/instagram.png" height="36" width="36" alt="instagram">
          <img src="images/facebook.png" height="36" width="36" alt="facebook">
          <img src="images/pinterest.png" height="36" width="36" alt="pinterest">
        </div>
    </div>
</footer>
```

7. Save the file.

8. Return to the browser to reload **index.html**. Scroll down to the footer. Lovely. Now let's float these icons to the right.

9. Return to your code editor. You should still be in **index.html**. Take a moment to look at the social media icons you pasted in the footer around line 36. They are in a div that has a class called **social**. We can use this to write the appropriate style.

10. Switch to **main.css**.

11. Add a new rule to the bottom of the styles as follows:

```
.wrapper {
   max-width: 1280px;
   margin-right: auto;
   margin-left: auto;
}
.social {
   float: right;
}
```

12. Save the file.

13. Return to the browser to reload **index.html**. Hmm. Not what we were hoping for. What's happening here? Let's inspect these elements in the browser.

    NOTE: The following steps are written for Chrome's DevTools, but if you decide to use another browser, the steps will be similar.

14. **Ctrl–click** (Mac) or **Right–click** (Windows) on the copyright paragraph and choose **Inspect**.

15. If it's not already highlighted, scroll over the **<p>** tag to see how it's highlighted in the browser:

The paragraph is a block-level element. This means it takes up the full width of the footer. So, the social media icons are floating—they are at the far right side of its parent container—but they are underneath the block-level paragraph. When we used the same technique in the header, our layout worked because the logo image is an inline element. It did not take up the full width of the header, so there was room for the rest of the navigation.

If we want the social media icons to pull to the right of the copyright paragraph, we need to investigate how the order of the markup really matters when floating elements.

16. Return to your code editor and switch to **index.html**.

17. Move the copyright paragraph so it goes **after** the social media icons:

```
<footer>
   <div class="wrapper">
      <div class="social">
         <img src="images/twitter.png" height="36" width="36" alt="twitter">
         <img src="images/instagram.png" height="36" width="36" alt="instagram">
         <img src="images/facebook.png" height="36" width="36" alt="facebook">
         <img src="images/pinterest.png" height="36" width="36" alt="pinterest">
      </div>
      <p>© hipstirred LLC</p>
   </div>
</footer>
```

18. Save the file and return to the browser to reload **index.html**. Wow! It worked. Why is that?

    You might recall that we used the float property in an early exercise to create text-wrap around an image. This works because not only does float move an element to the far left or right side of its parent container, the browser also pulls any content that comes **after** the floated element up and around to one side of the floated element. Essentially, in this case, the copyright paragraph is wrapping to the left side of the social media icons.

    In order to accomplish this desired wrapping effect, the browser takes the floated element out of the normal flow of the page. This means elements go from stacking on top of each other to sitting next to each other, given that there is enough room in the parent container.

More About Floats

In this particular project, we don't run into any undesirable layout issues but floats can get pretty tricky. When the browser takes a floated element out of the normal flow of the document, elements that stack below the floated area or wrap around the floated area can "collapse."

We cover everything you need to know about floats in the Web Development Level 2 class. For now, we recommend you check out the following resources:

alistapart.com/article/css-floats-101

css-tricks.com/all-about-floats

CSS Buttons & Floats

Simple CSS Buttons

We'd like the sign up link in the nav to be a prominent call-to-action. Ideally, the link should look and feel like a bright, eye-catching button. With the power of CSS background-color, padding, and border-radius, we can get the job done nicely.

1. Return to your code editor and switch to **main.css**.

2. Add the following new rule above the rule for .hero and below the rule for footer p, as follows:

```
footer p {
   margin: 0;
}
.button {

}
```

3. Give the .button rule a bright background-color:

```
.button {
   background-color: #a42821;
}
```

4. Save the file.

5. Switch to **index.html** in your code editor.

6. Add the **button** class to the sign up link, as follows:

```
<ul>
   <li><a href="#">about us</a></li>
   <li><a href="#" class="button">sign up</a></li>
</ul>
```

7. Save the file.

8. Return to the browser to reload **index.html**. This needs a bit of work. The text is too dark for the background and we need to add padding to the button to give it some girth.

9. Return to your code editor and switch to **main.css**.

10. Add the following new properties to the rule for .button:

```
.button {
   background-color: #a42821;
   padding: 10px;
   color: #fff;
}
```

11. Save the file.

12. Return to the browser to reload **index.html**. This is starting to really look like something. Let's round the button's corners using the CSS property border-radius.

13. Return to your code editor.

14. Add the following new property to the rule for **.button**:

```
.button {
    background-color: #a42821;
    padding: 10px;
    color: #fff;
    border-radius: 4px;
}
```

15. Save the file.

16. Return to the browser to reload **index.html**. Rounded! But we could fine-tune the padding a bit.

17. Return to your code editor.

18. Update the padding property declaration for **.button** as follows:

```
.button {
    background-color: #a42821;
    padding-top: 6px;
    padding-right: 12px;
    padding-bottom: 6px;
    padding-left: 12px;
    color: #fff;
    border-radius: 4px;
}
```

19. It would also look nice if the text were uppercase. Add the following property to the rule for **.button**:

```
.button {
    ( CODE OMITTED TO SAVE SPACE )
    border-radius: 4px;
    text-transform: uppercase;
}
```

20. Save the file.

21. Return to the browser to reload **index.html**. Very button-y. There are a few things we still need to fine-tune with the nav, though.

Adjusting the Nav & List Item Styles

1. Return to your code editor.

2. Let's change the text in the nav to be smaller. The other link should also be uppercase. Find the rule for **nav** and add the following property declarations:

```
nav {
    float: right;
    font-size: 13px;
    text-transform: uppercase;
}
```

3. Add space between the links with some margin on the **nav li**:

```
nav li {
    display: inline-block;
    margin-left: 10px;
}
```

4. Save the file.

5. Return to the browser to reload **index.html**. Super. The navigation could be aligned a bit better with the logo, though. Let's add some margin on top of the list items.

6. Return to your code editor.

7. Add some top margin to the **nav li**:

```
nav li {
    display: inline-block;
    margin-left: 10px;
    margin-top: 12px;
}
```

8. Save the file.

9. Return to the browser to reload **index.html**. Looks very enticing. It's hard to resist clicking this button. Let's reuse the button class for another link just under the hero section.

Creating a Second Call to Action

1. Return to your code editor and switch to **index.html**.

2. Between the **hero** and the **main** sections, add the following link:

```
<div class="hero">
    <h1>Curated Coffee</h1>
    <h2>A monthly subscription to sustainable coffees</h2>
</div>
<a href="#">Get Your Sign Up Code</a>
<main role="main">
```

3. Save the file.

4. Return to the browser to reload **index.html**. Okay. A link. Let's make it look nicer.

5. Return to your code editor.

6. Add the button class to the new link:

```
<a href="#" class="button">Get Your Sign Up Code</a>
```

7. Save the file and reload **index.html** in the browser to preview the change. Looks pretty good except we still have the default underline here. It would also look nicer if it were centered in the page. Let's fix these things.

8. Return to your code editor.

9. Wrap the new link we recently added in its own division and give it a **call-to-action** class, as follows:

```
<div class="call-to-action">
    <a href="#" class="button">Get Your Sign Up Code</a>
</div>
```

10. Save **index.html**.

11. Switch to **main.css**.

12. Add the following new rule below the rule for **.button**:

```
.call-to-action {
    text-align: center;
}
```

13. While we're here, let's get rid of the underline in the button style. Add the following new property to the rule for **.button**:

```
.button {
    ( CODE OMITTED TO SAVE SPACE )

    text-transform: uppercase;
    text-decoration: none;
}
```

14. Save the file.

15. Return to the browser to reload **index.html**. The call to action section could use more margin.

16. Return to **main.css** in your code editor.

17. Add the following property to the rule for **.call-to-action**:

```
.call-to-action {
    text-align: center;
    margin: 40px;
}
```

18. Save the file.

19. Return to the browser to reload **index.html**. Who wouldn't want to get a sign up code right now?! Good job.

Optional Bonus: Fixing an Edge Case Issue

Most popular mobile devices are about 320 pixels or wider, but most browsers do not allow you to resize the window smaller than around 400 pixels. If someone were to view this webpage at a width more narrow than this, the layout really fails.

To test this out, we recommend you use Chrome. In Chrome, we can dock the DevTools to the right side, and then resize the content area as narrow as we like.

1. To open the DevTools window in Chrome, **Ctrl–click** (Mac) or **Right–click** (Windows) on the page and choose **Inspect**.

2. To change the docking position of the DevTools window, at the top right of the DevTools panel click the ⋮ button and choose **Dock to right** as shown below:

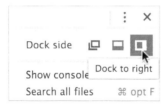

3. Now you can make the content area of the window as narrow as needed to test the code. You'll see how the navigation becomes difficult to see and interact with:

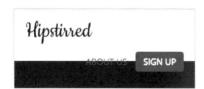

4. Let's return to **main.css** in your code editor to fix this.

5. Add the following property to the rule for **.wrapper**:

```
.wrapper {
   max-width: 1280px;
   margin-right: auto;
   margin-left: auto;
   min-width: 320px;
}
```

6. Save the file.

7. Return to Chrome to reload **index.html**. Much improved!

Exercise Preview

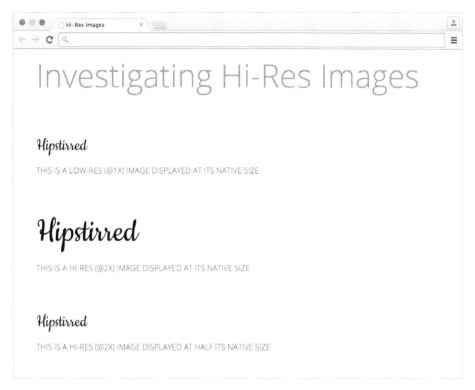

Exercise Overview

Some displays, like those on newer laptops and mobile devices, have a higher pixel density (smaller, more tightly packed pixels) than standard, low-res screens. These displays, which Apple calls **Retina**, but are also known as **HiDPI** (high dots per inch), typically have at least twice the number of pixels occupying the same amount of space on the screen. To provide crisp images for these devices, we have to use higher-resolution images.

1. We'll be using a new folder of provided files for this exercise. Close any files you may have open in your code editor to avoid confusion.

2. For this exercise we'll be working with the **Hipstirred Hi-Res Images** folder located in **Desktop > Class Files > yourname-Web Dev Class**. You may want to open that folder in your code editor if it allows you to (like Sublime Text does).

3. Open **hi-res-demo.html** from the **Hipstirred Hi-Res Images** folder.

4. Preview **hi-res-demo.html** in a browser. As the headings explain, we'll be placing both a low-res (@1x) and a high-res (@2x) version of an image in the browser to do some comparison testing.

6C   Hipstirred: Hi-Res Images

Sizing Things Up

1. Return to **hi-res-demo.html** in your code editor.

2. Add the following image just above the first **h2**, as follows:

```
<img src="images/hipstirred-logo.png" height="36" width="105" alt="Hipstirred">
<h2>This is a low-res (@1x) image displayed at its native size</h2>
```

3. Save the file and preview it in a browser. This is the logo we used in earlier exercises. We are viewing it at its native width, which is 105 pixels. If you have been working on a standard/low-res screen, this image is perfectly serviceable. If you have been working on a HiDPI/Retina desktop screen, however, you will have noticed then and now that it's a bit fuzzy and/or pixelated.

   To give users with hi-res screens the best possible experience, web designers export images at about twice the size at which they are intended to be displayed. Because these graphics tend to have 2 pixels for every 1 in a low-res graphic, they are typically called **2x** images. These images occupy the same amount of space as a low-res or **1x** image because the pixels are smaller. As an industry standard practice, hi-res images are saved with **@2x** at the end of their file name. Let's take a look at a @2x version of the logo image.

4. Return to your code editor.

5. Add the following @2x image just above the second **h2**, as follows:

```
<img src="images/hipstirred-logo@2x.png" height="72" width="210"
alt="Hipstirred">
<h2>This is a hi-res (@2x) image displayed at its native size</h2>
```

6. Save the file and preview it in a browser. As promised, it's twice as big! But we really only want this image to take up half as much space. How should we proceed?

Reference Pixels vs. Device Pixels

Pixels are a relative value. The size of a pixel completely changes depending on the pixel density of the screen. Luckily, we can use HTML and CSS pixels to declare the desired size of the element in the layout and the browser on any particular device will do the heavy-lifting for us to calculate the appropriate size of the element based on the available hardware pixels. HTML pixels and CSS pixels are often referred to as reference pixels because they provide the reference point for the device's browser to make the correct calculation based on the pixel density available.

1. We can see this in action. Return to your code editor.

2. Add the @2x image again just above the third **h2**, as follows:

```
<img src="images/hipstirred-logo@2x.png" height="72" width="210"
alt="Hipstirred">
<h2>This is a hi-res (@2x) image displayed at half its native size</h2>
```

We can set the pixel size in the code to half the image file's native size. This will end up displaying at the size we want, but at high resolution. This will appear the same size on low and high-resolution (HiDPI) displays, but they will look sharper on HiDPI displays. Let's try it out.

3. Edit the **img** size, as follows:

```
<img src="images/hipstirred-logo@2x.png" height="36" width="105"
alt="Hipstirred">
<h2>This is a hi-res (@2x) image displayed at half its native size</h2>
```

4. Save the file and preview it in a browser. If you are working on a hi-res screen, the @1x version of the logo on top will look slightly pixelated, but the logo will look sharper in the @2x version at the bottom. Success!

   NOTE: The hi-res @2x image will not appear sharper on low-res displays due to their limitations. Low-res displays are not technologically capable of showing the extra detail that HiDPI/Retina displays can show.

5. We can also use CSS to modify the size of a Retina or HiDPI image. Return to **hi-res-demo.html** in your code editor.

6. In the second version of the @2x image (above the third **h2**), completely delete the **height** and **width**, so you end up with the following:

```
<img src="images/hipstirred-logo@2x.png" alt="Hipstirred">
<h2>This is a hi-res (@2x) image displayed at half its native size</h2>
```

7. Save the file and preview it in a browser. The image is now rendering at its native width once more. Let's use CSS to set our desired size.

8. Return to **hi-res-demo.html** in your code editor.

9. Add the following class to the second version of the @2x image:

```
<img class="logo" src="images/hipstirred-logo@2x.png" alt="Hipstirred">
```

10. At the bottom of the embedded **style** tag (in the **head** of the file), add the following new rule:

```
   .logo {
      width: 105px;
   }
</style>
```

11. Save the file and preview it in a browser. Works like a charm.

6C Hipstirred: Hi-Res Images

Replacing Low-Res Images with @2x Versions in Hipstirred

1. Return to your code editor and open **index.html** from **Hipstirred Hi-Res Images**.

2. Let's replace the logo with the provided @2x image. In the **header** tag near the top, edit the logo image as follows:

   ```
   <img src="images/hipstirred-logo@2x.png" height="36" width="105"
   alt="Hipstirred">
   ```

3. Let's also replace the social media icons in the footer. Scroll down to the **footer** and add **@2x** to the images (as shown below). TIP: Some code editors (such as Sublime Text) let you create multiple cursors by holding **Cmd** (Mac) or **Ctrl** (Windows) as you click, so you can add this code to all of them at once!

   ```
   <img src="images/twitter@2x.png" height="36" width="36" alt="twitter">
   <img src="images/instagram@2x.png" height="36" width="36" alt="instagram">
   <img src="images/facebook@2x.png" height="36" width="36" alt="facebook">
   <img src="images/pinterest@2x.png" height="36" width="36" alt="pinterest">
   ```

4. Save the file and preview it in a browser. If you're working on a standard, low-res screen, there will be no visible change but if you are working on a hi-res screen—or your users have a hi-res screen—the logo and social media icons will look sharper!

   NOTE: We recommend leaving **index.html** open in the browser, so you can reload the page to see the changes you make in the code.

5. Now for the background image for the hero section. We've also a provided @2x version of this image. Return to your code editor.

6. Open **main.css** from **Hipstirred Hi-Res Images**.

7. Find the rule for **.hero** (near the bottom) and edit the **background-image** value as follows:

   ```
   background-image: url(images/hero-flat-white@2x.jpg);
   ```

8. Save the file.

9. Return to **index.html** in the browser and reload the page. Nice! But how do you know this is actually a retina image, particularly if you're working on a standard/low-res display? It works too seamlessly. Let's investigate.

10. Return to **main.css** in your code editor.

11. In the rule for **.hero**, comment out the **background-size** property as follows:

```
/*background-size: cover;*/
```

NOTE: A comment is a string of code within HTML and CSS that the browser ignores. It is often a simple note a developer adds to provide information about the code but it can also be used to temporarily disable code for testing purposes. Comments in CSS are written like this:

```
/* this is a comment */
```

Comments in HTML, however, are written like this:

```
<!-- this is a comment -->
```

If you are using Sublime Text, you can select code you wish to comment and hit **Cmd–/** (Mac) or **Ctrl–/** (Windows) to toggle comments on or off. Sublime Text will know if you are in CSS or HTML and write the appropriate comment syntax.

12. Save the file.

13. Return to **index.html** in the browser and reload the page. Woah. That's a big cuppa joe. So big, all you should see is part of the cup and saucer.

14. Return to **main.css** in your code editor.

15. In the rule for **.hero**, uncomment the **background-size** property to make the browser render it properly again:

```
 background-size: cover;
```

16. Save the file.

17. Return to **index.html** in the browser and reload the page. You are Retina ready.

Uploading to a Live Website via FTP

Exercise Preview

Exercise Overview

So far, the webpages you have built in class exist only on your local computer. To make your site visible to the world, the files must be placed on a web server. You can set up your own computer to act as a server but the safest, most common, and efficient way to publish your website is to use a web hosting service.

If you're taking a Noble Desktop instructor-led class, Noble Desktop will be your web host and you will be supplied with the connection information. If you are working from the book at your office or home, you can sign up for a free account with 000webhost.com on your own. If you create your own account, it's free and yours to keep, so it can be your first website if you don't already have one.

In this exercise, you'll use FTP (File Transfer Protocol) to upload a website to a web host's remote server so you can see how to take the work you've done on your local computer and actually put it live on the web.

FTP Clients

An FTP client is a software designed to transfer files back-and-forth between two computers over the Internet. It needs to be installed on your computer and can only be used with a live connection to the Internet.

While there are many great FTP clients you can use for uploading your website to a remote server, we chose to use **Cyberduck** in this workbook because it is free and cross-platform. Rest assured if you choose to use a different FTP client, it will involve the same basic steps we outline in the exercise: you drag your local files over to the FTP client window to put them up to a live, remote server.

6D Uploading to a Live Website via FTP

If You're in a Noble Desktop Instructor-Led Class

Noble Desktop will serve as your web host. The instructor will supply you with a username and password.

1. So you don't forget them, please note the following (you'll need them later):

   • Username

   • Password

2. Let's see how the website looks. Open a browser and type the following URL in the address bar: **http://192.168.1.254/yourUsername/** and hit **Return** (Mac) or **Enter** (Windows). This is just a default placeholder page, which you will be replacing soon.

3. Skip the section below and continue with the section titled **Getting Familiar with the Website & Customizing Content**.

If You're Working from the Book at Your Office/Home

1. Open a web browser and go to 000webhost.com

2. Click the **Free Sign Up** button on the right.

3. Under **Start Free Sign Up**, enter your **Email**, **Password**, and **Website Name** (subdomain). So you don't forget them, write them down (you'll need them later).

4. Click **Get Free Hosting**.

5. If you see it, fill out the CAPTCHA.

6. An email confirmation will be sent to you, so check your email now. Click the link in the email to confirm your registration and return to the 000webhost site.

7. In the dialog that appears, click **It's ok, I want to learn**.

8. Click the **Manage website "Website Name"** button.

9. Under **Build website** take note of your full **domain** (you'll need this later).

10. In the top-right corner, go into the **Settings** menu and choose **General**.

11. You will need the **FTP details** to upload your site. So you don't forget them, take note of the following (you'll need them later):

    • Host Name (should be files.000webhost.com)

    • Username

    • Password (same as website login password)

12. Let's see how the website looks. Under **Website Settings**, click the link to your website. This is just a default page—you will be replacing it shortly.

Uploading to a Live Website via FTP

Getting Familiar with the Website & Customizing Content

We'll be using a new folder of provided files for this exercise. This website folder contains the Hipstirred website with two final pages, including the index.html page you worked on in earlier exercises and an about.html page we have provided. Close any files you may have open in your code editor to avoid confusion.

1. Navigate to the **Desktop** and go into the **Class Files** folder, then **yourname- Web Dev Class** folder, and find **Hipstirred FTP**. Open the whole folder in your code editor if it allows you to (like Sublime Text does).

2. Open **about.html** from the **Hipstirred FTP** folder.

3. Preview the file in a browser.

4. You're about to upload the site but before you do, it would be nice to customize the content a tiny bit to make it your own. Scroll down to the second heading in the main content area: **How We Got Started**. Notice that there's a placeholder for your name.

5. Return to **about.html** in your code editor.

6. In the middle of the **main** tag, find the following paragraph:

   ```
   <p>YOUR NAME, Viv Kurt, and Max Mini were born...
   ```

7. Replace YOUR NAME with your own name.

8. Save the file.

Going Live

If you're working from your office or home, before proceeding, make sure you have downloaded **Cyberduck** from **cyberduck.io** and installed it. (Be sure to use the download link on the left, avoiding the ad at the top.) If you're in a Noble Desktop instructor-led class, Cyberduck has already been installed for you.

1. Launch **Cyberduck**.

2. Click the **Open Connection** button at the top left of the main window.

6D Uploading to a Live Website via FTP

3. Follow the instructions in the appropriate sidebar below.

If You're in a Noble Desktop Class

1. Next to **Server** enter **192.168.1.254**

2. For **Username** enter the username you selected or were assigned.

3. For **Password** enter the password you selected or were assigned.

If You're Working at Your Office/Home

1. Next to **Server** enter the **FTP Host Name** (files.000webhost.com) you wrote down earlier.

2. For **Username** enter the **FTP Username** you wrote down earlier.

3. For **Password** enter the **FTP Password** you wrote down earlier.

4. To connect to the server, click **Connect**. If you get a warning that you have an **Unsecured FTP connection**, just hit **Continue**.

   NOTE: If Cyberduck cannot make a connection, double-check your username and password and make sure there are no extra spaces.

5. Double–click on the **public_html** folder.

6. Once connected, you will see the window that lists the files for your site.

   TIP: Once connected, you can choose **Bookmark > New Bookmark** to save all this information for future use.

7. You are now ready to upload your files. In order to do this, move the Cyberduck window to one side so you'll be able to see your local file folder next to it.

8. Go to **Desktop > Class Files > yourname-Web Dev Class > Hipstirred FTP**.

9. Arrange this window and the Cyberduck window so they are side-by-side.

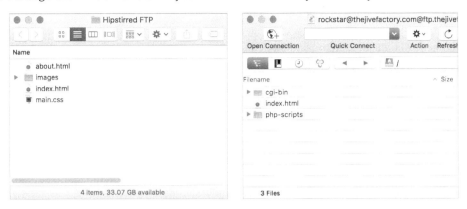

NOTE: The files depicted in the screenshot of the Cyberduck window may look different depending on your host. The screenshot in the book shows the file structure of the remote host only if you are at Noble Desktop.

10. When you upload your files to the remote server, it is called **putting** your files. This process is also known as **going live**. Let's do it. Click on the first file listed and then **Shift–click** on the last file in the list to select all your local files and folders.

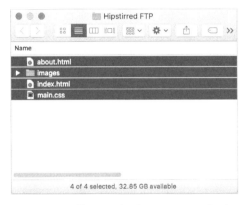

11. To **put** your files on the live site, simply drag the selected files and folders from your computer's window onto the Cyberduck window. TIP: Be careful to drop your files into the empty white space, NOT one of the existing blue folders.

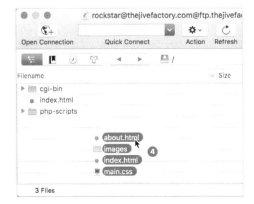

12. If you get another **Unsecured FTP connection** warning, just hit **Continue** once more.

13. A **Transfers** window will appear, showing the progress of the upload. (It may be running in the background.) If you get an **Overwrite** warning about overwriting the pre-existing index page, just hit **Continue** to overwrite those files with your own.

14. You can go ahead and close the Transfers window.

15. That's it, you have a live site! To see the remote files on the web, switch to a browser and go to:

• In Class: **http://192.168.1.254/username**

• Home/Office: **The domain you wrote down earlier**

NOTE: You may have to reload the browser to see the newly uploaded site.

16. Make sure to preview the about page to see your name. (Congratulations on your new startup, by the way.)

Making Changes

If you need to edit your website, you should first make changes to the local files on your computer and then upload them to the local server using FTP once more. Here is a brief recap of the steps to make your files live:

• Return to **Cyberduck**.

• If you are not still connected to your remote server, press the **Open Connection** button.

• Enter your **Server address**, **Username**, and **Password** and click **Connect**.

• Go into your computer, navigate to the local site folder, and arrange this window and the Cyberduck window so they are side-by-side.

• To upload the updated file, drag the file from your computer's window onto the Cyberduck window.

• If you want to upload more than one file, **Cmd–click** (Mac) or **Ctrl–click** (Windows) on each file and then drag them all over to the Cyberduck window. Additionally, if you click on one file and **Shift–click** another file, all the files in between them will also be selected.

The new files will replace the older files. Just remember, whatever you do to the live remote site happens instantly and CANNOT be undone, so upload carefully!

Form Basics

Exercise Preview

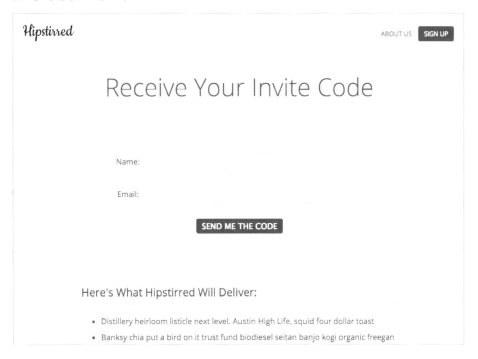

Exercise Overview

Forms allow you to collect information about your visitors so you can better serve their needs. In this exercise, you'll learn to code and style a basic form to collect a user's name and email.

Getting Started: The Form Tag

1. We'll be using a new folder of provided files for this exercise. Close any files you may have open in your code editor to avoid confusion.

2. Navigate to the **Desktop** and go into the **Class Files** folder, then **yourname-Web Dev Class** folder, and find **Hipstirred Form Style**. Open the whole folder in your code editor if it allows you to (like Sublime Text does).

3. Open **signup.html** from the **Hipstirred Form Style** folder.

4. Preview the file in a browser. We'll create a form directly under the main heading into a provided **signup** division.

   NOTE: We recommend leaving the page open in the browser as you work, so you can simply reload the page to see the changes you make in the code.

5. Return to **signup.html** in your code editor.

6. Around line 25, write the following new code shown in bold to start the form:

```
<div class="signup-form">
   <form action="">

   </form>
</div>
```

For the form to be processed correctly, you must make sure to place all content inside the **form** tag. The **action** attribute specifies where to send the form data when the user hits the submit button. We'll leave it blank for now.

Adding Name & Email Inputs to the Form

Text fields are created with the input element. Let's add a couple to our form so we can request a visitor's name and email.

1. Inside the form tag, add the following code:

```
<form action="">
   <input type="text">
</form>
```

The **input** element specifies a field where the user can enter data. The **type** attribute specifies what kind of control the browser should create. The default value for this attribute is **text**, but we are going to specify this in our code as a best practice.

2. Save the file and return to the browser to reload the page.

   It works, but it would be nice to have the user know what to type here. Luckily, there's an element built for that exact purpose.

3. Return to **signup.html** in your code editor.

4. Add the following code above the input element, as shown in bold below:

```
<form action="">
   <label>Name:</label>
   <input type="text">
</form>
```

5. Save the file and return to the browser to reload the page.

6. Looks better, but click on the label that says **Name**. Nothing happens. It would be nice if the label were attached or "bound" to the input element.

7. Return to the code and make the following changes:

```
<form action="">
   <label for="nameField">Name:</label>
   <input type="text" id="nameField">
</form>
```

8. Save the file and return to the browser to reload the page.

9. Make sure to click on the label that says **Name**. Aha! Your cursor is now automatically placed in the input field. This is a usability improvement overall, and for users with visual impairments, screen readers will now know which text to announce for which input. Most browsers will also automatically highlight the field with a blue or yellow glow.

10. Return to **signup.html** in your code editor.

11. Add the following new attribute to the **input** element:

```
<input type="text" id="nameField" name="nameField">
```

While the ID you added earlier allows us to bind the label to the input, the **name** attribute will be used when sending the form data to a script that will process the form.

Now that we have this label and input functioning the way we want them to, let's copy the code and create a second input for email.

12. Select the following two lines of code:

```
<label for="nameField">Name:</label>
<input type="text" id="nameField" name="nameField">
```

13. Copy the code.

14. Paste the code directly underneath like so:

```
<label for="nameField">Name:</label>
<input type="text" id="nameField" name="nameField">
<label for="nameField">Name:</label>
<input type="text" id="nameField" name="nameField">
```

15. Edit the code you just pasted to make the following changes (in bold):

```
<label for="nameField">Name:</label>
<input type="text" id="nameField" name="nameField">
<label for="emailField">Email:</label>
<input type="email" id="emailField" name="emailField">
```

NOTE: There are almost two dozen values you can use to describe the type of input you'd like to use in a form. We're using **email** here to improve the usability of this form: the appropriate keyboard will show on a mobile device and it will be easier to validate this field. Other types of input values include checkbox, radio, submit, hidden, tel, time, and date, for instance.

16. Save the file and return to the browser to reload the page. Good. But the inputs go side by side and we'd rather have them stack in this form. Let's group each label and input in its own div. This will be a clean solution.

17. Return to **signup.html** in your code editor. Wrap the first label and input for **nameField** in a **\<div\>** as follows:

```
<div>
    <label for="nameField">Name:</label>
    <input type="text" id="nameField" name="nameField">
</div>
```

18. Do the same for the **emailField** label and input, as follows:

```
<form action="">
    <div>
        <label for="nameField">Name:</label>
        <input type="text" id="nameField" name="nameField">
    </div>
    <div>
        <label for="emailField">Email:</label>
        <input type="email" id="emailField" name="emailField">
    </div>
</form>
```

19. Save the file and return to the browser to reload the page. We'll need to fine-tune the spacing with CSS in a bit but this will give us a solid foundation for doing so.

Adding a Submit Button

We need an input that will allow a user to submit their info.

1. Return to **signup.html**.

2. Inside the form below the second **\</div\>** for the **emailField**, add the following code shown in bold below:

```
    </div>
    <button>Send Me the Code</button>
</form>
```

NOTE: You can also use an \<input\> element with the type set to submit, but we like the flexibility of using a \<button\> element. Both methods perform the exact same function but a \<button\> may contain HTML content, which can give you more options should you want to add \<em\>, \<strong\>, or even \<img\> tags.

3. Save the file and return to the browser to reload the page.

    Let's make this form look a bit nicer. Remember to leave the page open in the browser, so you can simply reload the page to see your CSS modifications.

Form Basics

Styling the Form, Input, & Label

1. Return to your code editor and open **main.css** from the **Hipstirred Form Style** folder.

2. Scroll down to the bottom of the style sheet. You'll see that we've provided some extra styles. There's also a comment on the bottom. Below the comment is where you can write styles for the form you just coded.

3. Let's start by creating a visual delineation for the form, so it stands out a bit more. Add the following new rule:

```css
/* form styles */
form {
    padding: 60px;
    border: 1px solid #ddd;
}
```

4. Save the file and return to the browser to reload **signup.html**. Better. Now let's give the nameField and emailField some more breathing room.

5. Return to **main.css** in your code editor.

6. Add the following new rule below the rule for **form**:

```css
input {
    width: 80%;
    padding: 10px;
    margin-bottom: 30px;
}
```

7. Save the file and return to the browser to reload **signup.html**. Nicer. The width makes the inputs easier to see and interact with, the margin puts some space between the two fields, and the padding opens up the input so the user will have more space to land the cursor and type. The inputs could be prettier, though.

8. Return to **main.css** in your code editor.

9. To round the edges of the fields, add the following property to the rule for **input**:

```css
input {
    width: 80%;
    padding: 10px;
    margin-bottom: 30px;
    border-radius: 8px;
}
```

10. Save the file and return to the browser to reload **signup.html**. Okay, but the shading seems a little dramatic and dated. Let's flatten the look.

11. Return to **main.css** in your code editor and add the following to the **input** rule:

```
input {
    width: 80%;
    padding: 10px;
    margin-bottom: 30px;
    border-radius: 8px;
    border: 1px solid #ddd;
}
```

12. Save the file and return to the browser to reload **signup.html**. Much nicer. The labels are a little cramped next to the inputs, though. And the alignment of the content in the form might look better centered. Let's adjust this.

13. Return to **main.css** in your code editor and add the following to the **form** rule:

```
form {
    padding: 60px;
    border: 1px solid #ddd;
    text-align: center;
}
```

14. Add the following new rule below the rule for **input** as follows:

```
    border: 1px solid #ddd;
}
label {
    margin-right: 10px;
    margin-bottom: 4px;
}
```

NOTE: On a wider screen, the label sits to the left of the input, so margin is needed on the right. On a smaller screen, the label sits above the input so a bit of bottom margin is necessary.

15. Save the file and return to the browser to reload **signup.html**. Make sure to preview the form at a narrow width in the browser. The bottom margin doesn't appear to work. That's because **label** is an **inline** element. To fix this, we can set the label to display as **inline-block** instead.

16. Return to **main.css** and add the following to the **label** rule:

```
label {
    margin-right: 10px;
    margin-bottom: 4px;
    display: inline-block;
}
```

17. Save the file and return to the browser to reload **signup.html**. Note the improved spacing in the form at a narrow width in the browser.

Form Basics

Styling the Button

Let's beautify the button. We already have a handy **.button** class we're using for the main call to action on the home page and the Sign Up button at the top right of the navigation. Let's reuse this for the form `<button>`.

1. Return to your code editor and switch to **signup.html**.

2. Find the **button** element and edit it as follows:

   ```
   <button class="button">Send Me the Code</button>
   ```

3. Save the file and return to the browser to reload **signup.html**. Okay. Close, but not quite what we want here. What's happening is that the browser has default styles for button elements. We need to override those defaults.

4. Return to your code editor and switch to **main.css**.

5. Add the following new rule below the rule for **label** as follows:

   ```
       display: inline-block;
   }
   button {
      outline: none;
      border: 0;
      font-size: 16px;
   }
   ```

   In addition to stripping off the default border, we are disabling the outline most browsers will place on the button when it's clicked and also, for good measure, increasing the font size for better legibility.

6. Save the file.

7. Return to the browser to reload **signup.html**. It looks much cleaner. But mouse over the button. Sadly, the cursor does not change to a pointer by default when it's rolled over a button element. Luckily, a little CSS can do the trick here.

8. Return to **main.css** and add the following to the **button** rule:

   ```
   button {
      outline: none;
      border: 0;
      font-size: 16px;
      cursor: pointer;
   }
   ```

9. Save the file.

10. Return to the browser to reload **signup.html** and enjoy the look and feel of your form. If you would like to make it functional, check out the bonus exercise **Submitting Form Data to a Server-Side Script**.

Exercise Preview

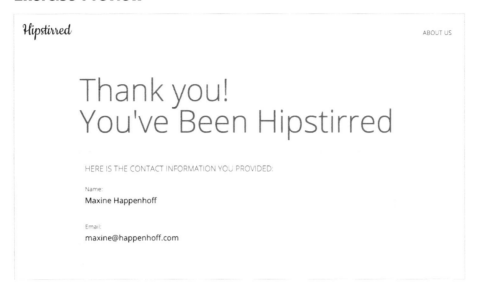

Exercise Overview

In this exercise, we'll show you how to submit the form to a script on the web server that will process the form information.

NOTE: If you are working at your office or home, we recommend you finish **Exercise 6D: Uploading to a Live Website via FTP**. At the very least, you must sign up for a free account at **000webhost.com** and write down your details for domain, login, file upload details, etc for use in this exercise.

Getting Started

1. We'll be using a new folder of provided files for this exercise. Close any files you may have open in your code editor to avoid confusion.

2. Navigate to the **Desktop** and go into the **Class Files** folder, then **yourname-Web Dev Class** folder, and find **Hipstirred Form Function**. Open the whole folder in your code editor if it allows you to (like Sublime Text does).

3. Open **signup.html** from the **Hipstirred Form Function** folder.

4. Preview the file in a browser. We marked up and styled this form in the previous exercise. Now it's time to give it some functionality.

Examining the PHP Script

We need a server-side form processing script to successfully collect the data we're requesting in the form. Scripting languages like PHP, ASP and Perl can be used to write a form processing script. Because PHP is supported on almost all web server platforms, we have provided a PHP script for you to use.

1. Return to your code editor.

2. In the **Hipstirred Form Function** folder, go into the **php-scripts** folder and open **form-handler.php** in your code editor. Take a look at the code. This is a super basic script that will store the user's nameField and emailField so they can be used in a variety of ways. For our purposes, this data will be sent to a "Thank You" landing page.

3. Note the following line of code around line 7, paying special attention to the code highlighted in bold:

   ```
   $landing_page = "Location: ".$_REQUEST['end_display'] ;
   ```

   Here is where the script will pass the information into a file that we'll specify as our **landing page**, so you can easily test the form action and see the user data. Note that the script requests an **end_display** variable. We will use this variable a bit later to point to the landing page from our HTML form.

   NOTE: On most websites, information submitted in a form is either sent as a plain-text email to the website owner or added to a database. On your own sites you would write your own script, hire a developer to write one for you, or use a third-party provider's script to process the information the way you want. For instance, if you wanted to have users sign up for your company newsletter, the Email Marketing Service you use (such as Salesforce, Campaign Monitor, or MailChimp, for instance) will provide you with a form code snippet that will interact with a script on the server side. You can style the form to match your site style.

4. Close **form-handler.php**.

Setting the Form Action

1. Return to **signup.html** from the **Hipstirred Form Function** folder in your code editor.

2. Find the **form** tag around line 25. Edit the value for the **action** attribute to point to the form-handler script, as follows:

   ```
   <form action="php-scripts/form-handler.php">
   ```

3. Save the file.

Submitting Form Data to a Server-Side Script

Adding a Hidden Field to Point to a Landing Page

Visitors will want to know when they have successfully submitted the form, so setting up a landing page is a best practice. For our purposes, this page will also allow us to quickly check the user data.

The landing page—thankyou.php—has been provided for you. It sits in the Hipstirred Form Function folder. As noted earlier, the PHP script has a variable called **end_display** to which we'll assign the value of the URL to our thankyou.php page. We can use a hidden field to do so.

1. Find the **\<button>** around line 34.

2. Add the following code (in bold) just below the button.

```
<button class="button">Send Me the Code</button>
<input type="hidden" id="end_display" name="end_display" value="../
thankyou.php">
</form>
```

3. Take a moment to review your code, checking the following:

   • Note that the type of this input is set to **hidden**. This means you will not see this if you preview the page in a browser (go ahead and give it a try if you like). This code is not hidden, however, to the script we'll use to process the form.

   • Double-check that you are using an underscore for **end_display**.

   • While you're at it, double-check the path to **../thankyou.php**. We need to include the **dot-dot-slash** prior to the file name since the PHP file that processes our form is in the php-scripts folder. This document relative path says to look up one level (to the root) to find thankyou.php.

4. Save the file.

Uploading & Testing the Form

We need to upload the form to the server to test it.

If you're working from your office or home, before proceeding, make sure you have downloaded **Cyberduck** from cyberduck.io and installed it. If you're in a Noble Desktop instructor-led class, Cyberduck has already been installed for you.

1. Launch **Cyberduck**.

2. If you chose **Bookmark > New Bookmark** to save your FTP information in an earlier exercise, you will be prompted to enter the password that you were assigned in an earlier exercise. Just enter the password and hit **Login**. You can skip the next step and move on to step 6.

   If you did not bookmark your FTP information earlier, follow the steps below.

3. Click the **Open Connection** button at the top left of the main window.

4. Follow the instructions in the appropriate sidebar below.

If You're in a Noble Desktop Class

1. Next to **Server** enter **192.168.1.254**

2. For **Username** enter the username you selected or were assigned.

3. For **Password** enter the password you selected or were assigned.

If You're Working at Your Office/Home

1. Next to **Server** enter the **FTP host name** you wrote down earlier.

2. For **Username** enter the **FTP user name** you wrote down earlier.

3. For **Password** enter the **FTP password** you wrote down earlier.

4. Under **More Options**, enter the path like so:
   Path: **/public_html**

---

5. To connect to the server, click **Connect**.

6. If you get a warning that you have an **Unsecured FTP connection**, just hit **Continue**.

   NOTE: If Cyberduck cannot make a connection, double-check your username and password and make sure there are no extra spaces.

7. Once connected you will see the window that lists the files for your site. You are now ready to upload your files. In order to do this, move the Cyberduck window to one side so you'll be able to see your local file folder next to it.

8. Navigate to **Desktop** and go into **Class Files > yourname-Web Dev Class > Hipstirred Form Function**

9. Arrange this window and the Cyberduck window so they are side-by-side.

10. Select all your local files by clicking on the first file listed and **Shift–clicking** on the last file in the list.

Submitting Form Data to a Server-Side Script

11. Drag and drop them on the **Cyberduck** window:

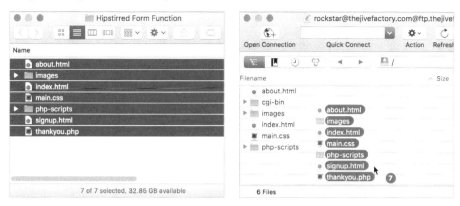

12. A **Transfers** window will appear, showing the progress of the upload.

13. If you get a warning that you have an **Unsecured FTP connection**, just hit **Continue**.

14. If you get an **Overwrite** warning about overwriting the pre-existing files or folders, just hit **Continue** to overwrite those files and folders.

15. You can go ahead and close the **Transfers** window.

16. When the file transfer is complete, switch to a browser and go to:

    • In Class: **http://192.168.1.254/username**

    • Home/Office: **Go to the domain you wrote down earlier**.

17. Navigate to **signup.html** from the link in the nav or the main call to action.

18. Fill out the form and hit the **Send Me the Code** button.

    Success! You will see the confirmation landing page. The form data has been processed and passed to the thankyou.php page.

    Normally that info would go into a database or get sent in an email, but in this case we've just passed it into a simple webpage so you can see that the form worked.

If the Form Did Not Work as Expected

If the form did not work as expected, there are two possible scenarios. The first is that nothing at all happened or you received a **404** file not found error. If that's the case, review the following instructions beginning with step 1.

If you were redirected to the thankyou.php page, but are missing the name or the email data, review the following instructions but skip to step 2.

B2

Submitting Form Data to a Server-Side Script

1. If nothing happens when you hit the **Send Me the Code** button to submit your data, most likely there is simply a typo in either the path to the PHP script or in the **hidden** field that points to the thankyou.php landing page. If this is the case, do the following steps:

   - Return to **signup.html** in your code editor.

   - Double-check the **action** attribute of the **form** tag. It should read:

     ```
     <form action="php-scripts/form-handler.php">
     ```

   - Double-check the **hidden input name** to make sure there is an underscore between end and display. Also check the value to make sure there is a **../** prior to the file name. The code should read:

     ```
     <input type="hidden" name="end_display" id="end_display" value="../
     thankyou.php">
     ```

   - Save **signup.html**

   - Put **signup.html** up to the server via **Cyberduck**.

   - Reload the webpage and try out the form again.

2. If the script worked but the name or the email data is missing, do the following:

   - Return to **signup.html** in your code editor.

   - Double-check the input names to make sure you haven't made any typos. The input for the user's Name should read name="nameField". The input for the user's email should read name="emailField". These are case sensitive. If you find a typo, make the correction.

   - Save **signup.html**

   - Put **signup.html** up to the server via **Cyberduck**.

   - Reload the webpage and try out the form again.

Spambot-Resistant Email Link

Exercise Preview

Exercise Overview

In this exercise, you'll learn how to create an email link so visitors can contact you. You'll also learn a best practice for hiding your email address from spammers.

Creating an Email Link Using the Mailto Protocol

1. We'll be using a new folder of provided files for this exercise. Close any files you may have open in your code editor to avoid confusion.

2. For this exercise we'll be working with the **Revolution Travel Contact** folder located in **Desktop > Class Files > yourname-Web Dev Class**. You may want to open that folder in your code editor if it allows you to (like Sublime Text does).

3. Open **contact.html** from the **Revolution Travel Contact** folder.

4. Preview **contact.html** in a browser to see what we have so far. Let's add the email contact information toward the bottom of the page.

5. Return to **contact.html** in your code editor and, around line 31, add the following bold code:

```
<p><strong>Phone:</strong><br>
   Toll Free: (800) Rev-Trav<br>
   Voice: (770) 272-7548<br>
   Fax: (770) 272-7558</p>
<p><strong>Email:</strong></p>
</main>
```

6. Let's put the email address on the line below **Email:** but still within the same paragraph. Add the following **break** tag and place the closing **</p>** on its own line as follows:

```
<p><strong>Phone:</strong><br>
   Toll Free: (800) Rev-Trav<br>
   Voice: (770) 272-7548<br>
   Fax: (770) 272-7558</p>
<p><strong>Email:</strong><br>
   </p>
</main>
```

7. Let's add the text our visitors will see:

```
<p><strong>Email:</strong><br>
   hello@revolution travel
</p>
```

8. There is a simple protocol for launching a mail application from a link. All you have to do is use the **mailto** protocol inside the href value to point to an email address and you've coded an email link. Add the following code to make your text a functional email link:

```
<p><strong>Email:</strong><br>
   <a href="mailto:hello@revolutiontravel.com">hello@revolution travel</a>
</p>
```

9. Save the file and preview **contact.html** in a browser.

10. Click on the link. If the computer is set up properly, it should launch an email program. If people visiting the website don't have an email program set up, or if they use web-based email like Yahoo mail, they'll still know the address by looking at the webpage.

Creating a Spambot-Resistant Email Link

There's a catch to using the mailto protocol. Spammers have email harvesters that scan websites and find these addresses. Luckily we can use JavaScript (a programming language used for interactive content on websites) to obfuscate the email link so spammers can't read it.

You can write a script that essentially breaks the **mailto** into pieces in the code and assigns nonsense variables to each piece. Email harvesters are rarely smart enough to understand the script and piece it back together, effectively hiding the address from spammers. If you were to Google **spambot-resistant email link**, you'll see that there are a ton of resources for you about writing your own script. There are even stock scripts you can edit and use, as well as online tools for generating a script.

1. We have provided a JavaScript snippet for you that's easy to edit and use in any project. Return to your code editor and open **spam-proof-email.html** from the **snippets** folder (in the **Revolution Travel Contact** folder).

2. Select all the code (**Cmd–A** (Mac) or **Ctrl–A** (Windows)).

3. Copy it (**Cmd–C** (Mac) or **Ctrl–C** (Windows)).

4. Close the file.

5. You should be back in **contact.html**.

6. Select the email link you just wrote (around line 32) and paste the JavaScript over it.

   TIP: In Sublime Text, to paste the code so it matches the current indention level, press **Cmd–Shift–V** (Mac) or **Ctrl–Shift–V** (Windows).

7. Edit the script by changing your-name to **hello** and your-domain to **revolutiontravel** as shown below in bold:

```
<p><strong>Email:</strong><br>
   <script>
      var eDone = 'hello'+'@'+'revolutiontravel'+'.'+'com';
      var eSubject = '';  // optional

      document.write('<a '+'hre'+'f="mai'+'lto:'+eDone+'?sub'+'ject='+eSubject
+'">'+eDone+'</'+'a>');
   </script>
</p>
```

8. The email's subject line can be prefilled by adding **?subject=Some Text Here** after the email address in a **mailto:** link. This is an option in our supplied JavaScript, so let's see how it works. Inside the single quotes, type **Travel Inquiry** as shown below in bold:

```
var eSubject = 'Travel Inquiry';  // optional
```

9. Save the file and preview **contact.html** in a browser.

10. If you are using **Internet Explorer**, you may get a warning bar that prevents you from seeing the email link. If you upload this page to a web server it will work, but for security reasons, IE prevents the JavaScript from working when previewed locally. To get the preview to work in **Internet Explorer**, you will have to choose **Allow Blocked Content** from the warning bar.

11. Click the email link. Wow! It works just like the mailto, but now it will be more difficult for spambots to harvest the email address. Notice it even has the custom subject line: **Travel Inquiry**!

12. When you are finished reviewing this page, close this file in the browser and in your code editor to avoid confusion while working through the remaining exercises in the book.

Designing Your Own Styles

Exercise Preview

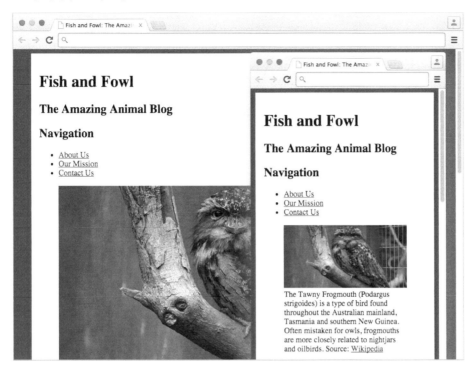

Exercise Overview

In this bonus, we'll return to the Amazing Animal Blog to add our own stylistic flair with CSS. Earlier in the workbook we coded a one page website about fish and fowl. While the structure is complete, and the page is fluid, it's stylistically drab. We'll use CSS styles to create a polished final product.

1. If you completed exercises 2D–3A, re-open **semantic-elements.html** (from the **Structural Semantics** folder). We recommend you finish the previous exercises (2D–3A) before starting this one. If you haven't finished them, do the following sidebar.

> ### If You Did Not Do the Earlier Exercises (2D–3A)
>
> 1. Close any files you may have open.
>
> 2. In your code editor, open **semantic-elements-with-sections.html** from the **Structural Semantics** folder.
>
> 3. Do a **File > Save As** and save the file as **semantic-elements.html**, replacing the older version in your folder.

B4 Designing Your Own Styles

Getting Started

1. Open **semantic-elements.html** in your browser. The webpage is structurally complete, but it's lacking personality. Let's use CSS to improve the visual appearance.

2. In your code editor, open **semantic-elements.html**. Slowly scroll down. Take a moment to review the code and make note of the different semantic sections.

3. Using CSS rules, give the webpage some character!

Tips & Ideas

- Modify the page colors.

- Make the section headers stand out with different font sizes, font family, or color.

- Get rid of the default bullet style for the list.

- Try making the navigation sit horizontally rather than stacking.

- Give the links interactive style with pseudo-classes.

- Use Google Web Fonts to give the page a unique logo.

- Put your styles in an external style sheet and link it in the webpage.

- Give the wrapper rounded edges using border-radius

- Test the mobile view using Chrome's emulator and adjust how the page scales.

Challenge: Building a Site from Scratch

Exercise Preview

Exercise Overview

It's important to practice your newly learned coding skills, so in this exercise we challenge you to build a small website without step-by-step instructions.

Getting to Know the Project

The site we challenge you to code is for **NAPS (National Association to Promote Siestas)**. In the **Web Dev Class** folder, you'll find a **NAPS** folder with the following:

- **images**: In this folder you'll find hi-res (Retina) quality photos and the NAPS logo. These have been optimized and are ready for use in the website.

- **page-designs-psd**: In this folder you'll find an editable Photoshop file for each of the four pages of the site.

- **page-designs-jpg**: In case you don't have Photoshop, in this folder you'll find a JPEG file for each of the four pages of the site.

- **text**: In this folder you'll find the text for each page, and the copyright.

Getting Started

We suggest you build the homepage first, and then move on to the other pages.

If you have Photoshop, open the Photoshop page design files (.psd). Inspect the various elements to learn type size, colors, etc.

B5 Challenge: Building a Site from Scratch

If you don't have Photoshop, refer to the JPEG designs instead. Because you can't inspect the various elements to learn about them, below we've included some of the specifications we use in the provided designs.

- Google Font: **Lato**

- Blue for the Navigation and Headings: **#00b0dc**

- Darker Blue for the Navigation's Bottom Border: **#009bc2**

- **Headings (h1):** Lato Bold, 34px size, 41px line-height

- **Sub-Headings (h2):** Lato Bold, 28px size, 34px line-height

- **Paragraphs:** Lato Regular, 17px size, 29px line-height

- **Large Paragraphs**: Lato Light, 24px size, 36px line-height

Check Out
OUR OTHER WORKBOOKS!

Web Development
Level 1 and 2

JavaScript & jQuery

GreenSock Animation

Mobile & Responsive
Web Design

WordPress

PHP & MySQL

Ruby on Rails

Photoshop for Web & UI

Photoshop Animated GIFs

Adobe Experience Design

Sketch

HTML Email

Responsive HTML Email

PowerPoint

Adobe InDesign

Adobe Illustrator

Adobe Photoshop

Photoshop Advanced

Adobe Lightroom

Adobe After Effects

Adobe CC: Intro to InDesign,
Photoshop, & Illustrator

NOBLEDESKTOP.COM/BOOKS

Listing on Search Engines

Once you create your site, you will want to be listed on the major web search engines. There are two types of listings: free and paid. If you are in a competitive field, you may need to pay to get listed well. However, it is possible with the use of strategic keywords that you can show up on Google, Bing, or Yahoo for free.

Before submitting your site to various engines/directories, you need to do a few things to the important pages on your site (those that you would like to be **indexed**, or found by the search engines).

Page Titles

Google will index the title of your pages and use those words as priority indexed words. In this case, the more information your title has, the better. For example, the title of your apple-picking farm website might be **Cornwall Farms**. But that does not mean anything to people who search the internet for **apple picking**.

What works better is this: **Apple Picking in New York State**

Try to make your titles as descriptive as possible, but keep them 60 characters or less. Difficult, yes, but that's the hand we have been dealt!

Meta Tags

<meta> tags go within the <head> tag to provide information on your page. There are a variety of meta tags, but the most important is the **description** tag. The description tag is what a search engine will usually display as the summary of your site. Another meta tag is the **keyword** tag. Unfortunately, it's virtually irrelevant now. Only Yahoo uses it at all, and even then, hardly. The best thing to do is create a keyword tag, just in case it IS ever used, and copy the description tag into it.

For more information on strategy to follow for better listings, check out searchenginewatch.com

Meta Tag Syntax

Here is an example of how the meta tags might look for an apple picking site:

```
<head>
<title>Apple Picking in New York State</title>
<meta name="description" content="Cornwall Farms Apple Picking in Upstate New York">
<meta name="keywords" content="Cornwall Farms Apple Picking in Upstate New York">
</head>
```

Listing on Search Engines

When someone performs a search, the site will usually show up in this context:

Apple Picking in New York State
Cornwall Farms Apple Picking in Upstate New York

The Submission Process for Free Listings

First, you should submit the pages you want indexed to Google and Yahoo/Bing. Compile a list of URLs that you want coming up in searches. Using Noble Desktop as an example, we'd want our **Web Development Certificate** page to be listed. Once you have a list of pages to submit, follow these steps:

1. Go to google.com/webmasters/tools/submit-url and submit your URLs.

2. Go to bing.com/toolbox/submit-site-url and submit your URLs.

Paid Placement

The big guns in paid search are Google and Bing/Yahoo. Around 75% of all web searches are done through Google and that is still growing. You may be amazed at the traffic that will immediately flow to your site after putting up a pay-per-click ad. Bing (by Microsoft) partnered with Yahoo and provides their paid advertising, so you only need to create accounts with Google and Bing.

Google

Google has a pay-per-click program that shows your ads above or next to search results and only costs you money if someone clicks on your ad. Go to google.com/ads and click on **Search Ads** to learn more and get started.

Bing

Microsoft's pay-per-click system works similarly to Google. We suggest duplicating your campaign from Google onto Bing and start measuring results. Go to bing.com and click on **Advertise** (at the bottom of the page) to learn more and get started.

Yahoo

Yahoo pay-per-click advertising is provided by Bing.

The Box Model Illustrated

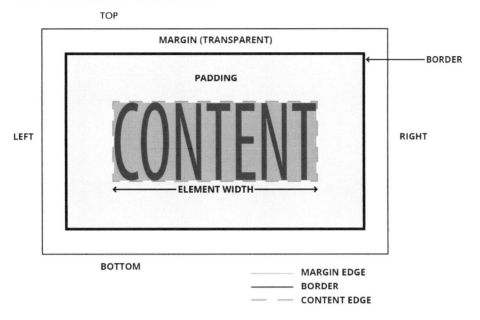

An important thing to note in the diagram above is that the width of an element is based on the content (text, image, etc.). That means when you add padding and borders, you increase the size of the element!

For instance, a 100px wide text block with 2px borders and 10px of padding is:

2px left border + 10px left padding + 100px width + 10px right padding + 2px right border = 124px total width of element

Padding vs. Margin Illustrated

In the example shown below, two paragraphs have the same style that has a gray background, black 1px border, and some margin and padding. The page's default margins have been removed so all the margin space you see is only from the style. We also beefed up the font-size so the paragraphs' text would be more legible.

Links to Reference Websites, Online Tools, & More

Because there are so many wonderful online tools, blog writeups, and more, we decided to make a site with all the links instead of printing them in this book. Not only does this save some typing, but it also will allow us to keep it more up-to-date.

Check out our suggested resources at **nobledesktop.com/webdev-links**
